WAINWRIGHT

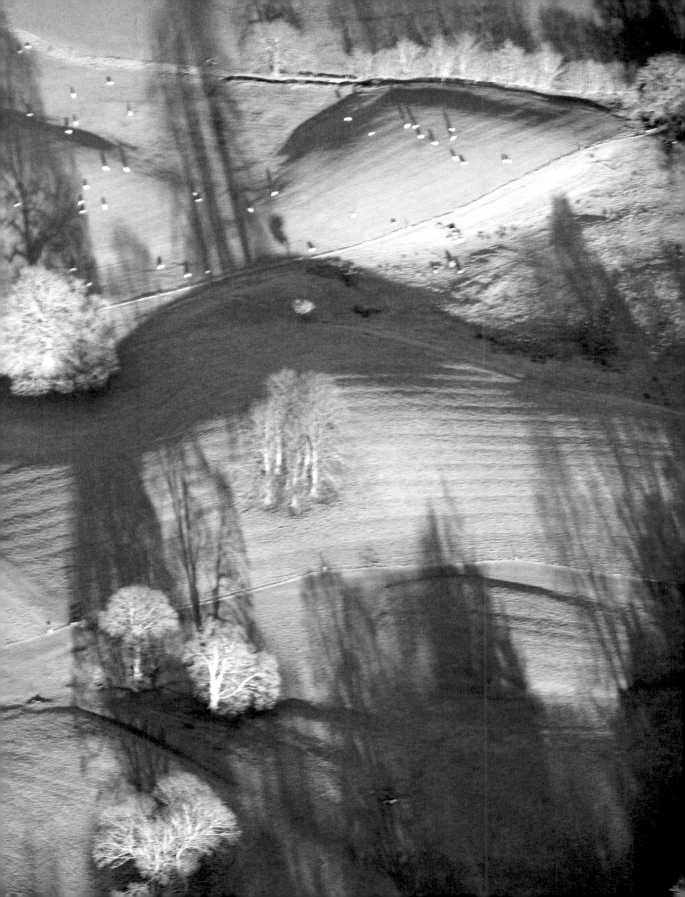

WAINWRIGHT

THE MAN WHO LOVED THE LAKES

Contents

Wainwright
The Life

Audley Range, Blackburn

FOR MORE THAN thirty years a solitary rambler tramped the highest and perhaps most beautiful land in England. He was tall, burly and often clumsy on the narrow paths and screes but he had a remarkable ability to vanish.

It was almost fey. Walkers would see him striding further up the track but when they rounded the corner there was only the smell of pipesmoke. 'Could that have been *him*, do you think?' they would ask one another. 'Someone said he was mapping this bit of the Lake District this weekend.' Then they would fish their Wainwright guidebooks out of their haversacks and sit down with an apple or some Kendal mint cake to check on the way ahead.

The man so many failed to meet was Alfred Wainwright, writer and illustrator of those very guidebooks, a child of the Lancashire cotton mill towns who was bewitched by the English Lake District when a young man. He walked for thousands of miles until, sated with pleasure, he sat in his attic study in Lakeland's little capital, Kendal, and began to write the fells a love letter which others might share. It turned into 47 books.

That on its own would be a monument worthy of the epic landscape of the Lake District, but these were no ordinary products of author, publisher and printing press. Handwritten in Indian ink, with guidelines and margins first ruled in faint pencil, the famous 'Wainwrights' are as beautiful in their own way as the mountains they describe. The 23-year-old who stood in a stunned silence on Orrest Head in 1930, awed by his first sight of a landscape which he at once compared to Heaven, bequeathed his own, unique gift to the national park. He is now a part of its history.

Above: View of Haystacks, with Buttermere and Crummock Water in the distance.
Above right: Alfred Wainwright. Overleaf: Easedale Valley near Grasmere

The beginning of this journey could scarcely have been less promising. Wainwright was born on 17 January 1907 into a two-up, two-down brick terrace house, 331 Audley Range, in Blackburn, which promptly became that much more overcrowded. The two bedrooms already housed his parents, Albert and Emily, and their older children Alice, who was 12, Frank, 10, and Annie, 7. The area was filthy with the smoke from cotton mill chimneys and the brickworks opposite, and the atmosphere at home was often thick with unhappiness too. Albert was a skilled stonemason, originally from the Yorkshire town of Penistone, in the Pennine hills west of Barnsley, but he was an alcoholic. He initially ran a quarry with his brother near Penistone, helped by money from their father who had a small but successful building business, but things went wrong. By

1907 Albert Wainwright was stuck in the Blackburn rut, only 37 but unable to get better work than short-lived stone-working contracts in the town. He earned enough to pay the 4/6d weekly rent (£82 at today's values) and provide the basics for the family and drink for himself, but there were no luxuries.

Emily, sweet-faced and as small and light as Albert was tall and thickset, was the daughter of an ironmonger in Penistone and a Congregational Sunday school teacher who retained her strong faith all her life. She took in washing and worked as a cleaner to supplement Albert's erratic wages, and tide the family over when he was out of work. Those were relatively good times, the couple's daughter Alice remembered in a family memoir written half a century later, because when her father had no money, he stayed sober.

Alfred also had no illusions about his father and revered his mother for the way she coped. In later life he remembered vividly the agonies he went through on Friday evenings when a woman in furs called for the rent and Emily sometimes had to ask for time to pay. 'I wished I was old enough to go to work to help my mother, or find a buried treasure,' he wrote in his autobiographical *Ex-Fellwanderer*. 'But there were no buried treasures in Blackburn in those days and none above ground either.'

The world beyond the Wainwrights' doorstep was the stuff of countless, ingrained images of the working-class North in Victorian and early 20th century years: tall chimneys, bleak streets, outside lavatories and still a knocker-up who clattered along the cobbles at 5am rattling on the bedroom windows with a pole. Cotton-spinning and associated trades – making the machinery, packaging and transport for textiles – swelled the town's population from 40,000 in 1844 to 130,000 in 1901 when Albert and Emily arrived, after brief and unsuccessful attempts to settle in Barnsley and Morecambe. Faces were often pinched and clothes handed down. Men wore clogs and women shawls over their heads, an interesting counterpart of the Muslim veils which may be seen in parts of Blackburn today. Factory hands had their wages docked if they were five minutes late on shift. And the factories were where everyone in Audley Range either worked or was destined to end up.

But not Alfred Wainwright. There was something a little different about him from the start. Uniquely in his family, he had thick, red hair. His mother used to hide her oddly coloured baby in a drawer when gossipy neighbours called, in case tongues wagged about his paternity. He resolved very early on that he would try to do something better and more exciting with his life, even if it wasn't likely to involve the adventures Jim Hawkins had on the high seas with Long John Silver and Ben Gunn. Alfred was to encounter R L Stevenson's *Treasure Island* and other descriptions of life beyond Blackburn later on at school, but he made an important discovery earlier than that.

When he was 11, his father bought him a rabbit and Alfred made a neat little drawing of the pet outside their hut in the terrace's 15-foot square back yard, with a careful list of its food, from grass and dandelions to potato and apple peelings. Two things stand out about the sketch and text which were done carefully in a schoolbook as classwork, kept for the whole of his life by Wainwright and now in his archive. The drawing is competent and fun, and the writing would earn gold stars for any modern 11-year-old. Encouraged by his mother, who regularly ate reduced portions or went without a meal altogether to make sure that her four children were well fed, he developed this talent for meticulous written work and closely observed sketches.

Above: The River Kent at Kendal. Opposite: A self-portrait, from The Far Eastern Fells by A. Wainwright

Attending Sunday School at Furthergate Congregationalist chapel introduced him to more of the wider and more brightly coloured world and, crucially, to maps. He started making his own of the Holy Land, at first copying from the missionary textbooks and then striking out freehand. Turning his attention closer to home, he produced beautiful and accurate maps of the North of England and its trades; fish in Hull, wool in Bradford, cotton in Blackburn and all the Lancashire towns round about. He quickly realised that the one-dimensional sheet of paper would draw extra interest and accuracy if its designer had a sound knowledge of the three-dimensional landscape which it portrayed. So he graduated to making his first solo walks into the centre of Blackburn, round its parks and,

as he entered his teens, onto the moors which encircle the town in its bowl.

Two central parts of Wainwright's character were thus established when he turned 13, the minimum school-leaving age at the time. He was devoted to his mother and the warmth and encouragement she gave him, which he was to try to rediscover in other women throughout his life. And he was very aspirational; no doubt in large part because of Emily's care and the contrasting wreck of his father's life, he did not accept the millhand mould into which so many of his friends would uncomplainingly fit. There was also a third important characteristic. Like his playmates, Alfred played Kick-the-Can in the street, kept caterpillars as pets in matchboxes and collected cigarette cards (which he also used as artist's

A. Wainwright: a self-portrait

material, copying the style of cartoons of famous cricketers to do sketches of his schoolfriends at Accrington Road Elementary). But he had his own particular and unusual hobbies, especially the making of lists. 'On wet nights I stayed indoors, sitting by the window, keeping a census of all who passed in various categories: pedestrians, cyclists, horses and carts.'

This strangely clerical hobby, which went with an aptitude for simple maths, earned him glowing reports at Accrington Road and at the Higher Elementary where he spent his last year, came top of the class and went home with a report studded with words such as 'Excellent'. Had there been money at home, a lad with 49/50 for English grammar and composition and 50/50 for maths would have gone on to Queen Elizabeth's grammar school. Instead, Alfred picked up a rumour that the Town Hall, near the Higher Elementary site in Blakey Moor street, was looking for an office boy. He applied.

Kendal Town Hall

In an essay in his last year at school on 'My Future', written as neatly as always on 8 March 1920, Alfred wrote: 'When I grow older, I fully intend to apply for a situation in an architect's office, or failing that, a position as an office boy in any other office... While in the office, I shall learn drawing plans and elevations, so that, besides learning useful knowledge on the subject, I should be able to carry on my masters' work, in case of illness.' The next step, he foresaw, would either be working as an architect or as a draughtsman at one of Blackburn's great foundries where he would pick up 'an idea as to inventory, and I may, later in life, get my fortune as an inventor. Who knows?'

This prophetic effort was only newly returned by Wainwright's teacher, inevitably marked

20/20, when a note arrived at 331 Audley Range from the Borough Engineer at the Town Hall. Alfred was offered, and unhesitatingly accepted, the very position as an office boy about which he had just fantasised. The headmaster of the Higher Elementary urged him to stay for another year to matriculate and have the chance of a county scholarship to further education. But Alfred had long ago thought this moment through. The grandeur of the Town Hall, with the golden ball on its clock which rose up a pole at midday and then slid down at 1pm to the sound of a gun fired from the building below, was irresistible. So was the 15/- a week (£90 today), of which he gave a handsome share to his mother. Even so, his pocket money rocketed from a penny to 1/3d

Above: Esk Hause. Above right: Wainwright memorabilia. Overleaf: Ullswater

(£7.50) a week. He recalled thinking proudly: 'I would now be able to go to a better cinema and attend Blackburn Rovers' matches instead of having to stand outside the ground trying to assess the scoring from the shouts of the crowd. This was affluence indeed; I was beginning to feel like a man.'

Wainwright was an immediate success in his new surroundings. He had a nicely understated sense of humour, which was later to flower in his books, and his ability to draw caricatures of his colleagues went down well. After three years' lowly apprenticeship among the engineers, he transferred to the Borough Treasurer's office at the age of 16. This was a better paid department staffed by brighter young men, many of them from the grammar school which only recently

had been far beyond Alfred's horizons. Wainwright was obliged to go to night school to cram for preliminary exams from which the grammar boys were exempt. Without passing, there was no getting on. Triumphantly, he sailed through them and a succession of higher exams until in March 1931 a telegram arrived at the Town Hall from the Institute of Municipal Treasurers and Accountants. Wainwright, A. had won the second highest mark in the country in that year's intermediate accountancy exams, the last before final, full qualification, and was to receive a prize. He had to go to the institute's annual conference in Brighton to collect it, a lightning expedition which left his views about the South of England as unenthusiastic as they had been, and were always to remain.

This was a time of early fulfilment and happiness in Wainwright's life. He had climbed the ladder, broken through the ceiling and flexed the intellectual muscles of which he had first become instinctively aware when he drew his rabbit and tabulated its diet 13 years earlier. Whatever his mild eccentricities and obsessions with lists and sums, he was popular with his colleagues. He had been told by his seniors that every page of his handwritten ledgers should be a work of art, and they were, but the skill involved was also put to lighter use. He wrote and illustrated a small, stapled booklet – only ever one copy made of each edition – called *The Pictorial Gazette* and sub-headed 'The unofficial organ of the accountancy office, Boro Treasurer's office'. Its pages were crammed with cartoons and jokes about the young would-be municipal accountants, including himself.

There were a handful of women in the office, too, and Alfred joined in the usual speculative chitchat with his male colleagues about their charms and possible sexual prowess. But when it came to reality, he proceeded in an awkward and unrealistically romantic way. Overhearing one young colleague whom he fancied, Betty Ditchfield, say that she was walking up the nearby landmark of Pendle Hill at the weekend, he went round the back of the outlying Pennine fell and was at the top waiting for her when she arrived. His pre-rehearsed gallantries would have been more appropriate for a knight engaged in medieval courtly love, and the encounter ended with him in tears, according to Betty years afterwards. With more self-confidence, he might have experimented more widely and learned to look more practically for a companion who shared or complemented his hopes and interests. But this was not to be.

In 1929 his sister Annie, who had gone into the mills in spite of a lively mind and appeals from her teachers to stay on at school, married her sweetheart from the brickworks in Audley Range. In the wedding photographs, which show Alfred with his red mop uncomfortably flattened by brushing ('It looked like he'd been hit on the head with a frying pan,' said Annie), a friend of the bride sits on one side with her cloche bonnet down almost to her eyes. She was Ruth Holden, a fellow hand at the cotton mill, and she was soon to be courting with Annie's younger brother.

Alfred's determination at work and perserverance with his art and writing had no parallel in the unpredictable sphere of human relations especially with young women, whose rules if any were a mystery to him. His assurance in his abilities, so sound in the office or exam room, dissolved. He wrote in *Ex-Fellwanderer*, many years later but still with feeling: 'I was not a good catch for any young female. I was shy, sensitive, skinny, ungainly. I had red hair and wore glasses. Who would have me?' When the answer emerged in hints from Annie's quiet friend, whose tugged-down bonnet was a way of concealing a mild cast in one eye, he was still more self-deprecating. 'Nobody ever regarded me with admiration. So when one at last showed an interest, I married her and left home, not easy in my mind and feeling that I was deserting my mother.'

It was a perilous start to married life, which began unspectacularly for the couple after a Christmas Eve wedding in 1931 followed by a 'honeymoon' evening at Blackburn's Star cinema and, a few months later, a move into a semi-detached house at 11 Hamer Avenue on a council estate near his parents' home. Wainwright had been keen to get away from the depressing presence of his father, but now, with one of those mismatches in timing which bedevil the best-laid plans, that presence was removed for ever. 'Six weeks after the wedding, my father died suddenly at the age of sixty two. My mother shed tears but there was no grief among the rest of the family. Had I foreseen this happening, I would never have left my mother and would have found a pleasanter house with a garden for both of us to enjoy.'

In spite of these ominous portents, the young

Wainwright at home c. 1970. Overleaf: Snow-bound ridge on Blencathra

Wainwrights appeared to prosper. They had a son, Peter, on 15 February 1933, and the following year became homeowners, quitting the rented council semi for their own corner house not far away, at 90 Shadsworth Road. Relatives remembered a lively atmosphere, with little Peter playing amid pets, a dog, a cat, a budgie, a tortoise and a mouse. Ruth made good, ample Northern teas and was an ace at picnics. Although a mill worker, she knew her countryside and could identify flowers, trees and birds. But relations, and Peter himself, recalled later that Alfred was often absent, doing overtime to continue his rise up the ladder at the Town Hall.

In 1941, when Peter was eight, something happened which baffled the little boy. His mother scooped him up and took him to live for a couple of months above an uncle's café on the edge of Blackburn's Queen's Park. Since the uncle had a plentiful supply of ice-creams and pop, Peter was content. But the episode, although ending in some sort of a modus vivendi and Ruth's return home, was the first overt sign that the marriage was in serious trouble. Unbeknown to anyone except Alfred, until after his death, secret proof of this had been committed to paper three years earlier.

Increasingly convinced that he could be a writer of more than municipal accounts and quips about colleagues, Wainwright privately wrote a fictional story about a man in agony at contracting a disastrous marriage, reproduced in full in Davies' biography. It was fiction only in name; the main protagonist was called Michael Wayne but his son was called Peter and his circumstances were all Alfred's. On his wife: 'She had tried so hard to please him before her affection for him had gone. Now she knew it was hopeless: she never would please him... She couldn't make him happy; it was beyond her power.' On his own attitude: 'He realized that his marriage had been a ghastly mistake; it had given him Peter, but nothing else. He had married someone who had been his equal. Now he had changed, for the better he thought. Certainly his aspirations were far nobler. But his wife had not changed with him. She never would. She was incapable of change.'

It is a heart-rending document which also contains two sentences which sum up the long, different kind of sentence which social convention as well as a common interest in providing a stable home for Peter, the one joy they shared, now imposed on the Wainwrights. 'There was no companionship, no comradeship. They lived together and were worlds apart.' It was a situation which continued for the next 40 years, while Alfred laboured steadily on at the office, first still in Blackburn where his wartime call-up was deferred, and then from November 1941 in Kendal. There he took a job as accountancy assistant, number three in the small town council's little financial hierarchy, and rose to become Borough Treasurer seven years later. He stayed in the job until 1967 when he retired at the age of sixty. And there the story might have ended, of a man as frustrated and depressed as 'Michael Wayne'. 'There were higher ideals, worthier ambitions. He should be striving for them. But they were not for him.'

Except... the misery of a loveless home was of great significance because it was to come to Wainwright's rescue in an entirely unforeseen way, and to play a fundamental role in the creation of his books. It all began the year before his marriage, when he persuaded a cousin to come with him on a trip beyond the immediate neighbourhood of Blackburn. It was his first adventure into what he regarded as 'another world, beyond reach, unattainable'. Which is to say that it was more than fifty miles from his home. The two young men chose the Lake District.

Derwentwater from Blencathra

Wainwright had read extensively about Macchu Pichu, Chimborazi, Cotopaxi and the rest of the world's alluring destinations. In his late teens, he and a friend had charted imaginary journeys in the Himalayas with strict topographical accuracy. He also knew plenty about the Lakes, culled from the respected Victorian guidebooks of M J B Baddeley as well as the great poets, Wordsworth, Coleridge and Southey. But nothing prepared him for what he saw when he reached the crest of Orrest Head, a modest hill above Windermere but one with a sensational view.

'Quite suddenly, it was as though a curtain had been dramatically torn aside... It was a moment of magic, a revelation so unexpected that I stood transfixed, unable to believe my eyes. I saw mountain ranges, one after another, the nearer starkly etched, those beyond fading into the blue distance. Rich woodlands, emerald pastures and the shimmering waters of the lake below added to the pageant of loveliness, a glorious panorama that held me enthralled. I had seen landscapes of rural beauty pictured in the local art gallery, but this was no painted canvas, this was real. This was truth. God was in his heaven that day and I a humble worshipper.'

Above: Alfred Wainwright on the fells he loved. Overleaf: Sunset at Walla Crag

Wainwright's cousin flopped on the grass in the sunshine and nodded off, while Alfred's mind continued in ferment. This was the day of the rabbit drawing, the day of the Town Hall job, the day of exam success writ many, many times larger. 'I was an alien here. I didn't belong. If only I could, sometime! If only I could! Those few hours on Orrest Head cast a spell that changed my life.'

Although the results of this change, which were to make Wainwright famous, did not take effect for many years, their genesis now began in earnest. From Orrest Head, Wainwright and his cousin tramped up the Troutbeck valley,

climbed their first mountain, Froswick, and marched on from its 2,359-foot summit along the lofty former Roman road on the spine of High Street. They stayed the night at beautiful, sleepy Howtown, then took the bus round Ullswater to Patterdale and clambered in sluicing rain over Striding Edge to the top of Helvellyn, third of the highest trio of mountains in England. The rest of the week saw them up in the North at Keswick and down south at Coniston. Wainwright returned to Blackburn with a sackful of annotated maps and a head full of plans for further forays into 'splendour far beyond my imaginings'.

Wainwright's house in Kendal

Again and again over the next 12 years, he was to explore as much of the Lakes as he could in weekend dashes from Lancashire, sometimes extended to a week with Peter, not just in Cumbria but also in the Yorkshire's Dales. But hardly ever with Ruth. If the Lake District may be considered a lover, Wainwright was consistently unfaithful in his marriage from day one. As the husk of the relationship became obvious, he thought less and less about his wife and more and more about the exquisite valleys, waterfalls and fells to the North. His supreme happiness was to bivouac high up in the fells, often hugging himself inside his overcoat to keep warm. It might be a dark, cold night but at dawn, for example after curling up on the 2,415-foot summit of Harrison Stickle: 'The scene I saw was the most beautiful I have ever witnessed. The tops were clear, although stark and sullen in the half-light, but below me the valley was completely filled by a white mist that extended from the steep upthrust of Rossett Pike at the dalehead and curved like an unbroken glacier, following the contours of the valley away into the distance over Elterwater and above the length of Windermere to the

Hallin Fell by Ullswater

sea, a mantle of unblemished purity. Far below, somewhere beneath the ceiling of mist, I could hear the cocks crowing. There were people down there in their beds who knew nothing of the glory of the morning. I stayed until the sun rose and coloured the peaks in a soft glow.'

The move to Kendal in 1941 was thus a Godsend. He was now in the county town of Westmorland and on the doorstep of Paradise. Although he might still feel an alien, because of one of the gaps which continued to puncture his growing self-confidence, he was at least no longer a visitor. His roaming became much more frequent and increasingly better organised; filling in gaps, re-surveying uncertain routes and making connections. Peter often went with him, the two of them plodding along in companionable silence, sometimes for as many as 38 miles in a single day. Wainwright wore his ordinary walking shoes and the oldest of his four suits. 'We walked slowly,' Peter recalled many years later after a buccaneering career overseas as an oil engineer. 'Typical of Civil Servants, doing everything slowly.'

Above: View from the boathouse on Rydal Water. Overleaf: The Rannerdale Valley

But while the Borough Treasurer stomped methodically over the mountains at weekends, away all day from his loveless home, his silence masked a mind working slowly but with mounting determination towards a Grand Plan. In the early 1950s, Peter got a trainee engineer's job at Kendal's gasworks after leaving school at 16 with eight decent O levels, and his father now roamed the fells entirely on his own. He thought increasingly about a book-length account he had written in 1938 of a fortnight's tramp from Settle in the Yorkshire Dales to Hadrian's Wall; it was a sort of precursor of much of the Pennine Way which Tom Stephenson was working out,

section by section, at the same time, an epic of route-making which became Britain's first long-distance national trail in 1965. Wainwright's manuscript was called 'Pennine Campaign,' and it was accompanied by what appeared to be a publisher's advertising pamphlet and reader's report. But no publisher had yet seen it (and one was only to do so in 1986, by which time its writer was famous, and it finally got into print). The pamphlet and reports were typical Wainwright skits, and the whole thing had been stashed in an envelope after being shown to a few close friends. Now, on 9 November 1952, a date he never forgot, he sat down to try again.

His plan was simple but immense. On his taciturn explorations, he had identified 214 distinct fells, or mountains, in the Lake District and he now proposed to climb, or re-climb, and describe them all. A series of books would chart in his own handwriting and with his meticulous maps and drawings, every route up the hills, the notable and curious features on the way, details of the summits and an orientation page of the views from them. He would travel only by public transport (he could not drive and never learned to); he had a rich store of knowledge about the fells already and he was a fit 45 – if somewhat overweight at 15 stone compared to nine and a half when he arrived in Kendal, thanks to Ruth's dutiful cooking. He had every weekend, some holiday and his now blessed lack of commitments at home. Applying his accountancy auditing skills to the task, he calculated that it would take him 13 years. At the end of the first, experimental, day, interrupted only by the hot meals which Ruth served up to very little response from himself, he was precisely on schedule: one page completed, on climbing 2,500 feet to the summit Dove Crag from Ambleside, which was a work of art every bit as much as a page of a guidebook.

Wainwright used thick artist's Indian ink, a mapping pen and high quality paper, the result initially appearing to be almost embossed with his gleaming black script and the dots and lines of the map. This was the template for every page which followed, in a style which had three hallmarks of his own. The handwritten text is the most obvious. When Harry Firth, the printing manager of the *Westmorland Gazette*, which was eventually to publish the series, saw a page of Wainwright for the first time, he said: 'I couldn't believe one man had hand-drawn every page. I don't think anyone since the days of the monks had produced a completely handwritten book.' His expert eye was also quick to detect the two styles, plain and italic, and two sizes, large and small, with which Wainwright varies the text, along with words or sections in the equivalent of bold type, created by pressing harder and slightly more broadly on the pen. These, and the irregularities in spacing which distinguish handwriting from type, add charm and variety to every page. Most readers take this in unconsciously but it can be rewarding to look closely and see just how many little human quirks there are. When a university's computer department tried to make a 'Wainwright' typeface to cut publishing costs, they were

unable to reproduce the effect. The only result was like a clever pattern monotonously reproduced on wallpaper. Wainwright's second innovation was his self-taught drawing style, which combined an almost photographic rigour with sly surprises. The basis of each illustration was a photograph, taken on his lonely wanderings in the style of an illustrious predecessor, Walter Poucher. Poucher was the Northern manager of Yardley's cosmetics and he combined his job with his hobby of mountain photography in an unusual way. Determined to wait until the weather was at its best for his pictures, he survived long and chilly vigils

by coating his face with Yardley's foundation cream. Many walkers in the 1950s reported seeing this strange apparition on the fells, and giving it a wide berth. Poucher needed to wait because his own guidebooks used an unusual style, printing clear photographs with a little wiggly line inked in white across them showing the route. Wainwright adapted this by taking the photo and then reproducing its basics in his Indian ink, with the dotted line of the route across them. He was very proud when one of the early letters complimenting him on Book One came from Poucher, who recognised a fellow perfectionist.

Above: The summit of Castle Grag. Above right: The disused quarry below Castle Crag's summit.
Overleaf: Boathouse on Ullswater, near Pooley Bridge

But Wainwright's drawings were not slavish copies of the photographs. Far from it. He included little details, sometimes drawn in an almost childish way; sheep whose anatomy was a bit suspect, miniatures of lead workings or oddly shaped rocks which nicely filled a gap in the text or an empty quarter of the map. Occasional walkers sneaked in too, usually shapely women who may well have been modelled on Betty Ditchfield, his impossible love back on Pendle Hill. And, always, one drawing per book of himself, sitting on a cairn, puffing on his pipe and, once, on a prehistoric mound with his sleeves rolled up and usually neat hair windblown, above the caption 'Ancient Briton'. The drawings were not usually of a quality to make them successful on their own, but they work brilliantly with Wainwright's text and maps.

The latter were his third idiosyncracy, using a patent style which has ensured the books' lasting value as practical guides, quite apart from their appeal as reading matter. Wainwright's decision to start the series in

1952 was galvanised by the publication of a new Ordnance Survey set of maps of the Lakes to a scale of two-and-a-half inches to the mile, much bigger than anything available before. He wrote lyrically about this as an historic moment for walkers and explorers, and dedicated his first book to 'The Men of the Ordnance Survey whose maps have given me so much pleasure, both on the fells and at my fireside.' His own maps were a combination of overviews of each fell, much like the OS's but even more detailed, and almost three-dimensional drawings of the route as seen from the side of the mountain, with features such as trees, dry-stone walls and hillocks standing out from the flat background. They pioneered the style now used with great clarity in ski guides, but with added humour. In a page on the ascent of Harter Fell which is girdled by forestry plantations, he sketched a 'Take Care not to start Fire' notice, adding that it would be a shame 'to waste all the effort spent in drawing all the little trees on this map'.

View of the Borrowdale valley

All these innovations in guidebook style were governed by one iron rule: perfection, or as near to it as a human being could get. Wainwright's absolute determination on this is shown by an extraordinary decision which he made in July 1953 when he had laboured for eight months and produced at least 100 pages. All of them were written in ragged text, which is to say that the lines were of varying length. It would look so much better, he decided, if the text was justified, with the beginning and end of every line exactly aligned as in most printed books.

He binned all 100 pages and started again, justifying the text on every page. It does not bear thinking about.

In an unpublished interview with *Cumbria* magazine after the publication of Book One, Wainwright used an appropriate metaphor for his relentless approach. He said: 'You remember the war maps, the black arrows of advancing troops, the pincer movements, the mopping up operations? That is the way I worked, but my thoughts were not of war, but utterly at peace.' By contrast, when it came to the business of

actually publishing the masterpiece, he was completely at sea. Knowing nothing about the subject, he enlisted his friend and colleague the Kendal Borough Librarian, a Cockney called Henry Marshall. Henry helped him find a local printer, Sandy Hewitson, whose bread and butter came from headed notepaper and small flyers, including regular orders for leaflets from the council. Sandy scratched his head at the bizarre idea of 2,000 copies of a handmade book, but got a sub-contracting quote from the much bigger *Westmoriand Gazette* and came

up with a price of £950 (£17,430 today). Wainwright had £35 (£650). 'Never mind,' said Sandy, who was one of the first people to be entranced by the sheer originality of the project. 'You can pay me when you sell them.' Wainwright acknowledged his debt handsomely in *Ex-Fellwanderer*. 'Sandy is dead now. He was kind to me. Kind men leave a gap when they pass on. The other sort are never missed.'

Sprinkling Tarn

The book appeared in May 1955 to an initially uncertain reception, partly caused by its author's extreme reluctance to publicise himself. This was the period when the legendary 'A.Wainwright' was born, the name preceded by a simple initial which became an object of mystery and therefore fascination among his growing number of readers for two decades until the truth emerged. Wainwright was genuinely self-effacing but he increasingly began to play up to the image of a grumpy Northern recluse who wouldn't even reveal his first name. By the time he wrote *Fellwanderer* in 1966, he was teasing his readers: 'The A can stand for Aloysius, if you want.' This was the heyday of cat-and-mouse games between the increasingly well-known writer and his pursuing fans. He describes a typical bout of fencing with a fan

Above: Stockley Bridge. Overleaf: Castlerigg stone circle. On page 44: Loughrigg Tarn, near Ambleside

on the summit of High Stile: 'She said, are you Mr Wainwright? No, I said. Well, she said, I know what he looks like and you look like him and I know he's working in this area at present; I do so want to meet him. I was a bit sorry then; my chances with the ladies were few and far between. No, I said again, but I know who you mean. Then off I went, and looking back later saw her leave the summit. I'm sorry, lass, whoever you are.' Out of kindness, he then gave the precise date, 26 July 1964, so that the woman might know that she had after all met her prey. He seldom lost the game, but 'Alfred' was eventually to be outed at the insistence of his publishers and TV producers when he had become a cult.

In the meanwhile, in 1955, sales were glacially slow to start with. A generous review in the *Lancashire Evening Post* by a fellow writer on the Lakes, the journalist and *Guardian* country diarist Harry Griffin, prompted only three orders in spite of the endorsement: 'I sincerely believe it to be the most remarkable book of its kind about the Lake District ever printed.' A full-page advertisement in Cumbria which had cost Wainwright £10 (£180) brought in a mere two more. Wainwright and Marshall had originally counted on the Whit weekend bringing plenty of customers to the Lake District's shops, just as the 12/6d (£11.50) book was beginning to go on show. Unfortunately a strike on the railways disrupted holiday traffic, and it was not until July that walkers and trippers arrived in earnest.

And then things changed. Wainwright's nervous watch on sales and thoughts about his enormous financial shortfall had been slightly eased by a review in the national *Guardian*, and a steady flow of very appreciative letters from friends and others who had bought the book. Now word of mouth began to do its work. By September, half the outstanding bill to Sandy had been paid and in February 1956 Wainwright called at the printworks with the final balance of £100 (£1,670). Two months later, Sandy ran off a second impression of

1,000 copies, this time with an enticing paper jacket which the first, cautious edition had been denied. When readers were offered a free jacket for their first editions, Sandy received more orders than the 2,000 books actually sold, and hundreds of advance requests for the next in the series and its successors. As Hunter Davies says succinctly in his biography: 'The cult of Wainwright had begun.'

Wainwright himself had meanwhile almost finished Book Two, establishing beyond doubt that he was in for the long term and not content to have produced one piece of excellence on which he could rest his laurels. In between his negotiations over printing and price, he had been marching up and down the Far Eastern fells and, in his self-declared role as a general with a huge, sweeping strategy, planning forays for Book Three on the Central Fells, Book Four on the Southern Fells, and beyond. The camera clicked, the pen dipped into the Indian ink, the presses rolled and the books sold. By 1962, when the penultimate Book Six was published, Book One had reprinted nine times, Book Two six, Book Three ten and Book Four nine. The following year, total sales topped £50,000 £700,000 today).

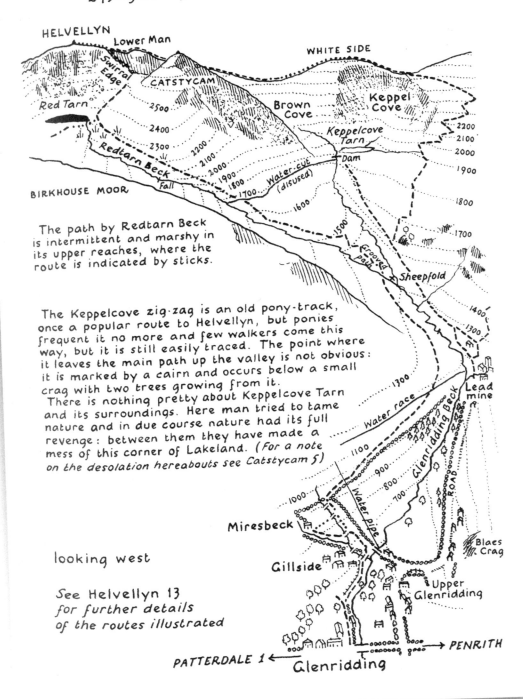

Helvellyn 16

ASCENT FROM GLENRIDDING
2750 feet of ascent : 4½ or 5½ miles

HELVELLYN

Lower Man

WHITE SIDE

Swirral Edge

CATSTYCAM

Brown Cove

Keppel Cove

Red Tarn

2500

2400

2300   2200   2100   2000

Keppelcove Tarn

2200
2100
2000
1900

Redtarn Beck

BIRKHOUSE MOOR

1900 1800 1700

Fall

Water-cut (disused)

Dam

1800

1600

1500

1700

The path by Redtarn Beck
is intermittent and marshy in
its upper reaches, where the
route is indicated by sticks.

Grooved path

Sheepfold

1400

1300

The Keppelcove zig-zag is an old pony-track,
once a popular route to Helvellyn, but ponies
frequent it no more and few walkers come this
way, but it is still easily traced. The point where
it leaves the main path up the valley is not obvious:
it is marked by a cairn and occurs below a small
crag with two trees growing from it.
There is nothing pretty about Keppelcove Tarn
and its surroundings. Here man tried to tame
nature and in due course nature had its full
revenge: between them they have made a
mess of this corner of Lakeland. (For a note
on the desolation hereabouts see Catstycam 5)

1700

Water race

Lead mine

1100

900

800

700

GLENRIDDING BECK

ROAD

1000

Water pipe

Miresbeck

Blaes Crag

looking west

Gillside

Upper Glenridding

See Helvellyn 13
for further details
of the routes illustrated

PATTERDALE 1 ←   Glenridding   → PENRITH

Facing page: 'Ascent from Glenridding', from The Eastern Fells by A. Wainwright. Above: Derwentwater with Keswick and Skiddaw in the distance

You can sense from the subtly changed style as the *Pictorial Guides to the Lakeland Fells* progressed that Wainwright was increasingly delighted that one 'noble aspiration' of his boyhood was coming true. His initial tendency to write slightly awkwardly in the style of conventional guidebooks relaxed, and he allowed more of his character and mannerisms to come through. Each book is preceded by an opinionated introduction and ends with a conclusion which links skillfully to plans for the next volume. Wainwright began to make jokes about his clumsiness on tricky stretches, to berate foolish behaviour by other walkers he encountered and to allow himself brief fantasies, where fells converse with one another, or he thinks about that nagging need of his own, a dream woman to share his life, especially on his lonely high-altitude bivouacs. Such references

brought a response from readers which in turn increased his playfulness, particularly when the fans appeared to be personable and intelligent women. One of them was the Cumbrian writer Molly Lefebure, who conducted such an entertaining correspondence with him that Wainwright suggested publishing it. They were not to meet for 13 years after the first letters were exchanged in 1957, but within weeks the Borough Treasurer was adopting an intimate style. Molly remembers: 'In one letter he asked if I was broad-hipped, as he liked broad-hipped women. I said I was thin, which I was at the time, and my hips were not at all generous. He then started leaving chocolates for me, the joke being that I was undernourished and needed feeding. When he was out working on the Guides, he would hide a chocolate bar for me, and give me clues where it was.'

In the final volume, Book Seven, published in 1966, Wainwright extended this treasure-hunting opportunity to all his readers, announcing that he had hidden a florin, or two shilling piece worth £1.25 today, under a flat stone four feet from the Ordnance Survey column on Lank Rigg. Characteristically, he refers to this as 'the only exciting experience to have occurred in the column's lonely life'. He sent one of the first copies of the book to Molly with a scribbled dedication –'To Molly, because I like her'– and a note saying: 'Quick, Molly, get your boots on. I want you to be the one to find the treasure.' But she was beaten to it by a man from Seaton near Workington, who started off from home the day after publication, at dawn.

Something else of enormous importance had also happened to Wainwright in the meanwhile,

which encouraged the sun to come out more frequently in his life as well as his books. In 1957 a slender, attractive young woman with a six-year-old daughter in tow was summoned to the Kendal Borough Treasurer's office to explain why a ten shilling fee for the hire of a Town Hall room by the local branch of Save the Children had not been paid. Unbeknown to either of them at the time, Alfred Wainwright's dream companion had made her first appearance in his life. She was Betty McNally, who had come to the Lakes to bring up her two daughters alone after separating from her husband, a doctor in Dublin. She always remembered her brief meeting with the Treasurer and his gentle reprimand for what was basically a muddle involving a fund-raising ballet show which had over-run and a grumpy caretaker who upset those involved in the surly way he demanded

overtime pay. The smell of pipe tobacco stayed with her, as it did with those walkers whom Wainwright eluded on the fells, and she recalls that after she said something complimentary about his guidebooks, she sensed 'a gentleness behind a stern front'.

It was not until seven years later that Betty met Alfred again, when she bought the latest of his *Pictorial Guides*, sent a fan letter and got an immediate reply which compared her comments to the first primrose of spring and suggested that she call by some time to chat about the fells. The women Wainwright liked made a lasting physical impression on him, and he had not forgotten the brief ten shilling chat. He said as much in his letter. Betty hesitated for a while but then bobbed into the Town Hall for an enjoyable natter on 20 September 1965, another of the dates in Wainwright's

life which he considered Momentous with a capital M and never forgot. Two days later, he asked her to call again by appointment at his office, where he handed her a large envelope, saying mysteriously: 'You are the girl.' He had taken the dramatic step of giving this chance, fleeting acquaintance his long-shelved story about Michael Wayne and his dream woman, accompanied by this note: 'Just read the book first, and make sure it is not a case of mistaken identity with me, and mistaken impression with you. Wait a fortnight, please. Then let me know.' It was an extraordinary repetition in many ways of his misconceived gallantries on Pendle Hill with Betty Ditchfield. But this time the outcome was different.

Because the new Betty had sensed something too. They might appear an odd couple, he large, 58, and coming up for retirement, she petite, 43, and bringing up two lively girls. But she replied in due course that something had been stirred in her by Wayne's story. She announced that she had picked the nickname 'Red' for her new friend on account of his hair, and consented to an increasing correspondence and regular meetings. Thus began a time of growing happiness for the lonely accountant and solitary walker, and one which was to last. The courtship went on for more than three years and was never easy, with Wainwright jealous of Betty's instinctive warmth towards others, including an eligible American visitor who unwisely discussed with Alfred his own hopes of married bliss with Betty. There were two divorces to weather, hers simple but Wainwright's messy. When Ruth eventually discovered his new relationship, she finally considered her duty as a wife done and left home, a separation of two mismatched people which went dismally but without a shouting match. Wainwright received a letter explaining the basics of running the house, in which he had never shown any interest: 'Coal will come once a fortnight unless you cancel it... Defrost fridge once a week... If electric clock stops turn the little nob (mispelt) at back right hand side.' They never met again, but lawyers sniffed possibilities in Wainwright's likely wealth from his books, which he had never discussed with Ruth. She eventually decided to contest his divorce application with one of her own and in June 1968 she won. Wainwright was found guilty of mental cruelty and had to pay a lump sum of £4,000 plus £500 a year for the rest of Ruth's life.

The court heard convincing evidence that he had been, in Ruth's words, 'selfish, withdrawn, sullen, refusing to converse for long periods of time'. He had also 'shown scant and increasingly less interest in her, her happiness and general well-being, and had regarded her as being but a housekeeper, domestic worker and convenience'.

It was the dark side of the man, foreshadowed in the story of Michael Wayne, and the more believable because it was sometimes shown to others. Henry Marshall, for instance, never received the credit he deserved from Wainwright for running the publishing business before the *Westmorland Gazette* took over. He had done all the chores the writer disliked or did not understand. But because Wainwright did not understand them, any more than he did the defrosting of the fridge or ordering coal, he seemed not to acknowledge the work and self-sacrifice involved.

For the man himself, this dark side was now banished completely by Betty McNally; not only through her attractiveness and vivacity, but because she had a Volkswagen Beetle which played an important part in his next literary step. For the *Pictorial Guides*, Wainwright had stuck absolutely to buses, telling Hunter Davies when they first met: 'The slower the bus, the better I liked it. There's nothing more restful than a stopping bus.' In those days, he had no reason to hurry home, quite the opposite. But now he did, and his new books also took him out of the Lake District into the vast tracts of the Pennines where few buses ventured. In some of the filthiest weather for a long time, he set out in 1966 to tramp, map and write about the 270 miles of the Pennines threading across the hills, and an awful lot of peat bog between Edale in Derbyshire and Kirk Yetholm just the Scottish side of the border.

It was one heck of a slog, and by the end of it he lugubriously addressed readers who might follow him, in his customary Personal Conclusions section to the *Pennine Way Companion*, which followed the model of the *Pictorial Guides to the Lakeland Fells*. 'You won't find me anywhere on the Pennine Way. I've had enough of it.' There was a certain amount of stage grumpiness in this, because even in mucky weather and claggy mud, Wainwright relished a solitary tramp. It was a signal mark of his feelings for Betty that when

Preceding pages: Blencathra. Above: Ullswater. Overleaf: Wasdale Head and Pillar

she asked if she could come with him on a walk he grudgingly agreed. She recalls the turning point: 'One day I threatened I was going to follow him, walking behind. Eventually he agreed, but on one condition. "As long as you don't talk," he said.' But although the walk added to the gradual national awareness of his work because of his rash promise to stand a free pint of beer to everyone who finished it, at the Border Hotel in Kirk Yetholm, he was relieved when it was over. By the time of his death, the Border Hotel stunt had also cost him more than £15,000.

The second walk was completely different and has become a memorial to Wainwright which is almost as dearly loved as the *Pictorial* *Guides to the Lakeland Fells*. In 1967 he began to tease out a long-standing ambition, a marathon path created by his own exploration and map-reading, composed of interlinking rights of way. He considered the Lakes, the Yorkshire Dales and even Scotland, but then had the inspiration of crossing the North from coast to coast through three national parks and tracts of lonely or seldom visited countryside in between. The Coast to Coast walk has become one of the most popular in the country, actually bringing modest economic revival to some of the tucked-away places on its 192-mile route, such as Cleator in the former mining rim of western Cumbria and Danby Wiske in the flat heart of North Yorkshire's Vale of Mowbray.

Betty's presence is no longer ignored but celebrated in Wainwright's charming *A Coast to Coast Walk*, which acknowledges in its Introduction: 'Everybody has a car these days, even me (and in my case, a good-looking competent chauffeur to go with it.)' The book is full of cheerful throwaway compliments to women, in contrast to some of the churlish things he had to say in the Lake District guides, such as his remark suggesting that old mineshafts on Wetherlam fell might be full of 'the mingled remains of too-intrepid explorers, sheep, foxes, dogs and women whose husbands have tired of them'. Indeed Wainwright more or less dedicates the path to women at the end of his Personal Notes in Conclusion. 'The Pennine Way is masculine; the Coast to Coast Walk has feminine characteristics. If there happens to be something in your temperament that makes you like the ladies the odds are that you will prefer the C to C. You may not meet any but you will be reminded of them. On the PW, you never give them a thought… well, hardly ever.' The *Coast to Coast* also made up, to some extent, for a weakness of the Lake District guides which has often attracted criticism over the years. Many experienced ramblers such as Harry Griffin of *The Guardian*'s Country Diary felt that they were too detailed and killed all the adventure of the hills. Wainwright's topography was so exact that the walker literally turned right at a particular tree and left at a specified stone. The *Coast to Coast* is not like this. Wainwright specifically urged his readers to try their own routes, following his technique of 'pathfinding' in the literal sense of the word. There was no need to follow slavishly his *Coast to Coast*. Hundreds of alternative routes awaited explorers with good map-reading skills along the way. So it has proved. In the Vale of Mowbray, for instance, Wainwright trudged a full eight miles along metalled roads, back lanes but still roads, because farm paths were overgrown or blocked. Today, there is no need to walk any road at all after determined reconnaissance by the great man's disciples.

Above: Ashness Bridge near Derwentwater in Borrowdale

He also continued in a long-established vein of contempt for prescriptive lists of things which all walkers should wear or carry with them, a dislike of nannying which also helped to reconcile his views with those of Griffin and other mountain men. Typically in *Fellwanderer* Wainwright writes: 'You see hikers setting forth for a day on the hills burdened as though they were starting a six months' expedition to Antarctica: they are grim and anguished of face when they ought to be carefree and smiling. They are not going into uncharted wastes and should have no more sense of apprehension or impending risk than if they were going for a Sunday afternoon stroll in the park. The hills are friendly: there are no lurking hazards, no traps around every corner. The dangers have been absurdly exaggerated; there are too many gloomy prophets around, and too many people ready with advice. You are not making a date with death. You are not making a technical excursion into space. You are going for a walk.' By the mid 1970s, Wainwright was indeed becoming a Great Man, at least in the terms of publishers and the media. It had taken a long time, but word had got round in London's influential circles that there was this extraordinary publishing phenomenon in faraway Kendal. At the heart of it was that

Overleaf: View of Eskdale Valley from Harter Fell. On page 60: View of Fleetwith Pike from Buttermere

type beloved of journalists and PR people, a mystery man. The more that Alfred tried to hide away behind the anonymous A.Wainwright – sometimes obscured even more into the lamely witty A.Walker – the more determined they became to flush him out.

The first success went to Michael Joseph in the early 1980s, who finally persuaded Wainwright to make the move away from handwritten books. After the *Coast to Coast*, he had produced a series of delightful successors to the Pictorial Guides dealing with peripheral hill country: *Walks on the Howgill Fells, Walks in Limestone Country, The Outlying Fells of Lakeland* (for the

increasingly elderly like himself). But he was beginning to tire of the intense work involved, and he also had a motive for earning more money. Apart from his payments to Ruth, he was developing a long-cherished plan to build a shelter in the Lake District for abandoned dogs and cats. It was partly play-acting, in his role as cussed old misanthropist, but he genuinely enjoyed the uncomplicated affection given by pets. Book Three of his *Pictorial Guides* had been dedicated to 'The Dogs of Lakeland' as long ago as 1958.

By the early 1980s, his royalties had raised more than £30,000 (£86,000 today) for the area's animal charities, but his favourite, Animal Rescue, needed twice as much as that to get a properly equipped centre built. It was at this pivotal moment that Michael Joseph's suggestion of a series of 'coffee table' books arrived in the post. They were to be written by Wainwright with illustrations by the much-admired photographer Derry Brabbs, plus a good helping of Alfred's drawing and maps. It was partly a recycling job so far as Wainwright's input was concerned, but the ten books were handsomely successful, covering the Lakes in several volumes, Scotland, the Pennine Way, the Yorkshire Dales and the Coast to Coast. Wainwright never completely dropped his scepticism, warning Michael Joseph at one stage that sneerers were predicting that the next in the series would be 'Wainwright on the

Lay-bys of Lakeland'. But the books have sold over 700,000 copies and Wainwright's many new experiences during their making included his first visit to a Little Chef restaurant, where he ate three gooseberry pancakes in a row.

Galvanised by the effect on his earnings for the animal shelter, he also embarked – to his friends' amazement – on television work, first in a successful regional programme, where much of his brief debut was obscured in a cloud of pipesmoke. Then began a hugely successful series of stolid, snail's pace pottering about in the hills with Eric Robson, the broadcaster from Radio 4's *Gardener's Question Time* who also ran a sheep farm in lonely Wasdale. They had a very funny time from the moment they met at a 'get to know you' lunch in Keswick where Wainwright ordered fish and chips, as always, while Robson had a healthy ham salad. Halfway through the meal a stealthy

hand removed a slice of ham from Robson's plate. The hand was Wainwright's, and the ham was stolen for his cat, Totty. Wainwright played up to his laconic image on camera and produced many classic Northern Grumpy reflections such as: 'It's a wonderful world, as Louis Armstrong told us, but it would be more wonderful without a lot of the people in it.'

The five programmes were extremely successful, attracting three million viewers each to BBC2 in 1986 and prompting two further series of ten programmes in all. Wainwright even agreed to go to London for a press conference, the first time he had been to the capital for 20 years, since being invested with an MBE at Buckingham Palace for his *Pictorial Guides to the Lakeland Fells*. This was not a concession he was prepared to make for his next and perhaps most prestigious media outing: an appearance on *Desert Island Discs* with Sue Lawley in his eightieth year. The celebrated Radio 4 programme had tried to tempt him before, but the demands of Animal Rescue had been less pressing at that time, and Roy Plomley did not have the attributes of Lawley which appealed to Wainwright's romantic side. He laid down the absolute condition, however, that he would go no further south than Manchester to meet her. To Lawley's relief, the administrators at Broadcasting House agreed. The recording was a memorable exercise in laconic Northern bluntness, particularly when Lawley asked Wainwright if he blamed his wife for walking out on him. Bearing out the verdict of the divorce court 18 years earlier, he replied: 'Not at all – I don't know how she stuck it for 30 years. Right, what's your next question?'

Above: Wainwrighta and pipe. Facing page: 'Signing off.', from The Southern Fells by A. Wainwright

The publicity on TV and radio sent the sales of Wainwright's books rocketing, and by the end of 1990 Animal Rescue had more than £350,000 (£530,000 today) in the bank. At last, the boy from Blackburn felt that he could afford to relax. As Hunter Davies says: 'His life was a long, slow ascent up a path to a summit that he saw quite early on and determined to reach.' He had reached it, and as he told the TV cameras on his roamings with Eric Robson: 'I can face anybody now, and not feel inferior to them.' There had been some terrible mistakes on the way, hard words to people who did not deserve them and cruel, selfish treatment of the woman he should never have married. Crippled by rheumatoid arthritis, Ruth had died in a nursing home in 1985 and the miseries of the marriage had created a permanent distance between Alfred and Peter, the son for whom he had predicted such great things. Father and son rubbed along when Peter came back to England from working as an engineer with the Bahrain Petroleum Company for 15 years. But there were thankless memories of boyhood evenings in Kendal, when Peter's mother and he sat in silence by the fire, stuck in the sitting room because there was no heating elsewhere in the house, but forbidden to talk or have the television on because Father was doing his drawing by the inglenook.

But the noble aspirations had been achieved in other fields: the books above all, but also the animal shelter and the new life with the woman Wainwright felt he should have met so many years before. Wainwright's sisters and brothers had died, in age order, and he remarked on several occasions that his turn would be next. On 20 January 1991, that turn came and Alfred Wainwright died peacefully three days after his 84th birthday, confident in his reputation and content that his last wishes concerning the scattering of his ashes would be met. His favourite fell was Haystacks on the beautiful ridge between Buttermere and the lonely youth hostel of Black Sail, which he compares in his books to a shaggy terrier in the company of sleek foxhounds – the shapely summits of High Stile, Great Gable and Pillar.

'All I ask for, at the end,' he wrote in his autobiographical fragment *Fellwanderer*, 'is a last long resting place by the side of Innominate Tarn on Haystacks, where the water gently laps the gravelly shore and the heather blooms and Pillar and Gable keep unfailing watch. A quiet place. A lonely place. I shall go to it, for the last time, and be carried; someone who knew me in life will take me there and empty me out of a little box and leave me alone. And if you, dear reader, should get a bit of grit in your boot as you are crossing Haystacks in the years to come, please treat it with respect. It could be me.'

Wainwright

The Lakes

Keswick and Derwentwater from Blencathra

THE ENGLISH LAKE District was already well trodden when Alfred Wainwright dipped his pen in the Indian ink and began the first page of the *Pictorial Guides* in November 1952. Immortal literary figures had tramped the fells and valleys for inspiration and they unintentionally invented mass tourism as a result.

In grumpy middle age, William Wordsworth lamented the effects of the railway arriving at Windermere in 1844 with a poem which starts: 'Is there no nook of English ground secure from rash assault...?' But it was in large part his doing. Four years later and fifty miles south in her Pennine village, Charlotte Bronte described in surprise how 'folks come boring

to Haworth' to seek out the setting of *Jane Eyre* and *Wuthering Heights*. The phenomenon was writ large in the Lakes where Wordsworth and Samuel Taylor Coleridge's *Lyrical Ballads* were far from alone. Robert Southey and Sir Walter Scott were part of the romantic Lakes movement too, and so was Thomas de Quincey, who lodged at the Wordsworths' Dove Cottage in Grasmere and achieved the remarkable feat of editing the *Westmorland Gazette* in Kendal for 17 months from this then-remote valley.

This talented coterie absorbed the landscape into their work and crucially, like Alfred Wainwright after them, they lived among and loved the fells. Earlier writers had largely travelled through them and then fled back

Scafell Pike in the distant horizon

to London with exaggerated shudders. Their landscape was savage, mist-wrapped and – favourite adjective – 'horride', a place to be visited only by armchair in front of the fire. Not so the Lake Poets, who set out to beguile their readers with the notion of actually wandering lonely as a cloud through drifts of daffodils. They wanted everyone to discover what bliss it was to be alive in Cumbria, where to be young, or at least fit enough to climb the fells, was very Heaven.

'Heavenly' is the adjective most often used by Alfred Wainwright to describe the Lakes, where the concentrated beauty of mountains and valleys has so many subtle additions. The colours are ravishing, from the fresh greens of spring to autumn's tawny slopes of dying bracken amid the pale straw of mountain grass. The long and shapely lakes themselves act as mirrors of the hills and especially of the sky, notorious for its rain but as a result constantly changing, flecking the blue with clouds or mountain mist. There is no more exciting companion on the fells to the seasoned walker. Delicate veils come and go, golden with sunlight or tinted pink at dawn or dusk. Everyone in such moments can experience that ecstasy which overwhelmed Wainwright when he bivouacked overnight high in the hills.

Millican Dalton's 'Cave Hotel'

Around him was a rich variety of wildlife too, from humble creatures like the newt in Hard Tarn which engages so many readers of Book One, to the wraith-like shape slinking through the fir plantations in lonely Ennerdale, or at least through the imagination of many walkers there. The valley is one of the last places in England where the pine marten holds out, a fabulous encounter if you are very quiet and lucky. More likely is a meeting with the red squirrels which scamper between the oak trees in many quiet places, closely monitored by local people to protect them against the invasive greys. There are rare mountain butterflies, an entire flora of plants and, everywhere, the Herdwick and Swaledale sheep whose endurance of foul weather and unexpected agility on the crags fascinated Wainwright. He often draws them, both as anonymous woolly blobs to vary his hosts of miniature trees, and as characters engaging with the walkers who invade their world.

The sheep are not ornamental. For all its beauty and heritage of famous poets and writers, the Lake District is a working landscape. Its picturesque dry-stone walls have a serious purpose, and you do not have to venture far to find lunar landscapes left by quarrying and mining for stone, slate, lead, copper and the once fabulously rare graphite used for munitions as well as pencil-lead. Many fellwalking routes were originally farmers' and quarrymen's daily way to work. Navigating in mist across the featureless humps above Black Sail youth hostel, countless walkers have thanked God for Moses' Trod, a well-cairned track which skirts the dangerous precipices of

Great Gable. It is easy to forget as you edge down to safety that this was the workaday route for 19th-century quarrymen hauling sledges of slate to ships at Whitehaven and Barrow. Or for the eponymous Moses, who supplemented his quarryman's wages with an illegal still, hidden in the surrounding crags.

The working world has left its own beauty in the Lakes, especially in the well-husbanded intakes, or valley pastures, which look so neatly reassuring through those windows in the mist. At the centre of each settlement stands a long, low farm, grey stone but more often whitewashed, half of it used by the family, the rest for animals in winter and their feed and straw. Historically, these are the homes of Cumbrian 'statesmen', independent yeomen who escaped early from England's feudal yoke. There are only a few 'big houses' in the Lake District's countryside.

By contrast, the small resort towns have plenty. First the industrial barons of the North built their mansions in choice spots around the lakes and then mass tourism brought the mixture of gusto and tat which marks the holiday trade. That is now the lynchpin of the economy, far more important than farming, but it has its beauty too. The circular pepperpot home on Belle Isle of an 18th-century mining magnate, John Curwen, adds charm to Windermere. It is lovely to see the Ullswater steamers with their bright red funnels and trails of smoke, or the golden serpent figurehead of Gondola, the National Trust's Victorian yacht which putters round Coniston Water.

Two worlds then: the poets' and the everyday. But they often meet, and a fine symbolic example is the great rock known as Brothers' Parting, below Grisedale Tarn and the upper slopes of Helvellyn and Dollywagon Pike. Here William Wordsworth, poet, and his brother John, sea captain, shook hands in 1805 for the last time, before William wandered off for a day in the hills while John strode to Barrow and his East Indiaman the *Earl of Abergavenny*. She was to sink two weeks later in a storm off Portland Bill, drowning 300 passengers and crew including Wordsworth.

Brothers' Parting lay at the heart of Wainwright's proposed Book One, but first he had to set his orderly mind to the purpose of his proposed series and think about what gap it could possibly fill. The *Lyrical Ballads* had been published 164 years earlier and since then whole shelves, even libraries, of writing about the Lake District had followed. There were stacks of maps and drawers of geological, soil and agricultural surveys. Novels and poetry were two a penny — including Hugh Walpole's lastingly successful *Rogue Herries* chronicles. Nostalgic memoirs spilled out from local publishers and the Flopsy Bunnies reigned supreme over a nursery cupboard of children's books. Guides of variable quality gave details of everything from off-season B&B rates in Keswick to the time of the last bus from Coniston to Ambleside. Was there anything left to say?

There always is; and Wainwright had spotted two holes in the apparently blanket coverage. First, there was little if anything on the less favoured and often forgotten ways to reach the summits, each of which tended to have only one popular way up. Trippers were more or less herded up the likes of Skiddaw and Helvellyn or congregated at lower honeypots such as Easedale Tarn via tracks which were as big as minor roads. The skeletal remains of a café by Easedale Tarn show the scale of this cosy form of mountain tourism, as does the turnstile at the Lodore Falls in Borrowdale, where the local hotel pressed halfpenny reprints of Southey's poem 'How Does the Water Come Down at Lodore?' on all visitors. A stash of them was one of the assets when the place went bankrupt in the 1930s Depression. Like the Snowdon mountain railway, the tracks corralled visitors conveniently for the extraction of money, but for Wainwright they were a spur to seek out other, unfrequented paths.

Preceding pages: Grizedale and Ullswater. Above and facing page: Summit views of Haystacks, with Buttermere and Warnscale Bottom below

In one of the first routes in Book One, he describes the walkers' 'motorway' up the zigzags on the 2,810-foot Dollywagon Pike as 'tedious and thronged with recumbent pedestrians'. A couple of pages later, he is revelling in a solitary ascent of the Pike by the Tongue ridge above Ruthwaite Cove. 'This is much the most interesting and exhilarating way to the summit, but it is relatively unknown and rarely used.' But, or because? Such contrasts appear throughout the series, as Wainwright accumulates a matchless collection of lost paths: the overgrown, grassy horseshoes to the left of Rossett Gill's terrible plod up loose scree; the Fornside zigzags on an obscure flank

of the 2,870-foot Great Dodd which avoid 'the abominable marshes of the eastern slopes. It seems an oversight of nature that the sheep here are not born with webbed feet.'

Wainwright's second opportunity was the seldom explored Empty Quarter in the spaces between the paths, known largely to sheep, their shepherds and the occasional 'crag rat' climber looking for a rock face off the beaten track. The intricate folds of the Lake District mean that many of these hollows, hanging valleys and spurs to ridges are much more complicated than they look at a casual glance. Their treasures are hidden: rock pools for a summer swim, waterfalls by an emerald patch of grass with

Overleaf: **Ashness Bridge near Derwentwater in Borrowdale**

a rowan tree to shade the perfect picnic; caves once used by the likes of Moses of the Trod, cobwebbed mineral workings and obscure tarns. The big, burly man from Kendal Town Hall, with his haversack, camera and pipe, knew many of them from his two decades of lonely wandering. He wanted to map them all.

To prospect the lost routes and the lonely spaces between them, Wainwright had to divide the Lake District into manageable sections, a process which had challenged his predecessors but proved his first great success. Coleridge had decided on an enormous circle, a meandering loop which nearly ended close to his starting point when he tackled without any previous experience the dangerous rock climb of Broad Stand, which seals for walkers the route between Scafell Crag and England's highest mountain Scafell Pike. 'The jolt of the fall on my feet,' he wrote after dropping seven feet onto a narrow ledge above a lethal precipice, 'put my whole limbs in a tremble... I began to suspect that I ought not to go on but unfortunately though I could with ease drop down a smooth rock seven feet high, I could not climb back up it, so go on I must, and on I went... every drop increased the palsy of my limbs. I shook all over.' Wordsworth's *Guide* of 1820 also saw the Lakes as circular but approached them in a less dramatic way.

He compared the valleys and ridges to the spokes of a wheel – a crooked one but the metaphor was apt. Walter Poucher's guides then split the hills into the main massifs with their principal outriders, missing out many minor peaks in the process. Baddeley trawled the valleys conscientiously, but gave only summaries of paths to just twenty of the principal mountain tops.

Wainwright lassoed his own circle round all the ground over 1,200 feet, but turned it into the shape of an uncut diamond by straightening the edges into lines between the outer ends of nine radiating lakes plus the village of Caldbeck in the north, which he included to avoid missing out the final bastions of the hills before the Cumbrian plain and the Solway Firth. Other issues dear to his clerical mind then came into play as he cut his diamond into book-sized chunks. Dividing 214 chosen fells by seven produced the right average length for the sort of volumes he had in mind, each covering between 25 and 35 peaks. All were based on distinct mountain groups. Unlike those infuriating map series which divide in a vital area and consequently force you to buy more than one, the *Pictorial Guide*'s sections never overlap. You need only take one book at a time. The final result is a much more coherent version of Wordsworth's wheel. Book Three, *The Central Fells*, forms the hub from which the other six are spokes.

Each volume has a similar internal structure, based on its resident giant, the biggest mountain in the section, from which ridges lead to smaller companion peaks with outliers completing what amounts to a pyramid. The divisions vary a little; Book Four, *The Southern Fells*, embraces the highest of all the fells, the Scafell massif, and is therefore longer and better endowed with giants than Book Six, *The North Western Fells*, where only Grasmoor and Eel Crag top the 2,700-foot mark. But the principle is the same, and it gives the guides their feel and ease of use which is so distinctive.

INTRODUCTION

Classification and Definition

Any division of the Lakeland fells into geographical districts must necessarily be arbitrary, just as the location of the outer boundaries of Lakeland must always be a matter of opinion. Any attempt to define internal or external boundaries is certain to invite criticism, and he who takes it upon himself to say where Lakeland starts and finishes, or, for example, where the Central Fells merge into the Southern Fells and *which* fells *are* the Central Fells and which the Southern and *why* they need be so classified, must not expect his pronouncements to be generally accepted.

Yet for present purposes some plan of classification and definition must be used.   County and parochial boundaries are no help, nor is the recently-defined area of the Lakeland National Park, for this book is concerned only with the high ground.

First, the external boundaries.   Straight lines linking the extremities of the outlying lakes enclose all the higher fells very conveniently. There are a few fells of lesser height to the north and east, however, that are typically Lakeland in character and cannot properly be omitted : these are brought in, somewhat untidily, by extending the lines in those areas. Thus:

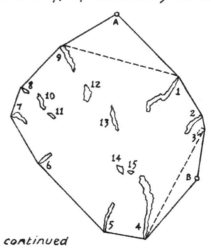

1 : *Ullswater*
2 : *Hawes Water*
3 : proposed *Swindale Res.*
4 : *Windermere*
5 : *Coniston Water*
6 : *Wast Water*
7 : *Ennerdale Water*
8 : *Loweswater*
9 : *Bassenthwaite Lake*
10 : *Crummock Water*
11 : *Buttermere*
12 : *Derwent Water*
13 : *Thirlmere*
14 : *Grasmere*
15 : *Rydal Water*
A : *Caldbeck*
B : *Longsleddale (church)*

continued

INTRODUCTION

Classification and Definition

continued   The complete Guide is planned to include all the fells in the area enclosed by the straight lines of the diagram. This is an undertaking quite beyond the compass of a single volume, and it is necessary, therefore, to divide the area into convenient sections, making the fullest use of natural boundaries (lakes, valleys and low passes) so that each district is, as far as possible, self-contained and independent of the rest.

This division gives seven areas, each with a well-defined group of fells, and each will be the subject of a separate volume

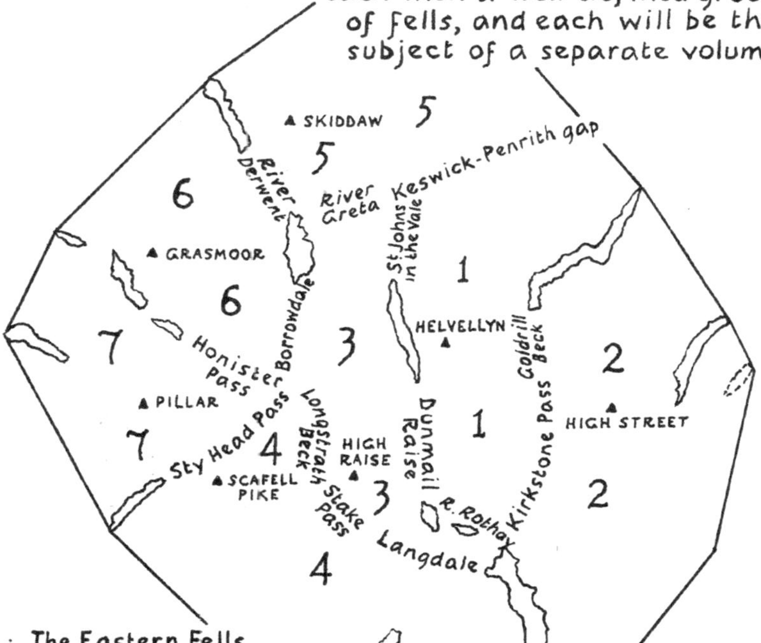

1 : The Eastern Fells
2 : The Far Eastern Fells
3 : The Central Fells
4 : The Southern Fells
5 : The Northern Fells
6 : The North-western Fells
7 : The Western Fells

Preceding pages: 'Introduction', from The North Western Fells by A. Wainwright.
Above: Aerial view of Kendal. Facing page: 'Natural Features', from The Eastern Fells by A. Wainwright

Wainwright started as he intended to finish, and he started very well. His choice for Book One was the area which he termed *The Eastern Fells*, whose giant is Helvellyn, at 3,118 feet England's third-highest mountain and the most often climbed of the Lakeland peaks. 'Legend and poetry, a lovely name and a lofty altitude' were part of its romance, wrote Wainwright, reflecting in his introduction that 'there is some quality about Helvellyn which endears it in the memory of most people who have stood on its breezy top. Although it can be a grim place indeed on a wild night, it is, as a rule, a very friendly giant. If it did not inspire its affection, why would its devotees return to it so often?'

The main reason is the challenge of the most exciting ridge in Lakeland for walkers, Striding Edge, which runs a narrow arête between Red Tarn and the desolate hollows of Nethermost and Ruthwaite Coves – themselves classic high-altitude byways which Wainwright encouraged his readers to explore. The Edge itself shrinks at one stage to narrow slabs where many prefer to creep along on their hands, knees or bottoms. It is described in detail in Walk 2, but it is only one attraction of a sprawling mountain which had many others for Wainwright to record. Establishing another unique characteristic of the series, Book One has dozens of quirky observations inserted between the maps, drawings and text. They point out for example the abundance of hazelnuts in Dovedale and the large population of voles on the eastern flank of Nethermost Pike, and make it clear that this is going to be a series whose focus will be intense. Baddeley described the 20 most popular summits; Wainwright has 14 different ways to climb Helvellyn alone and he remains the only guide writer to note the hidden presence, 500 feet from the summit, of Brownrigg Well, a natural spring of ice-cold water available all the year round.

Helvellyn 3

NATURAL FEATURES

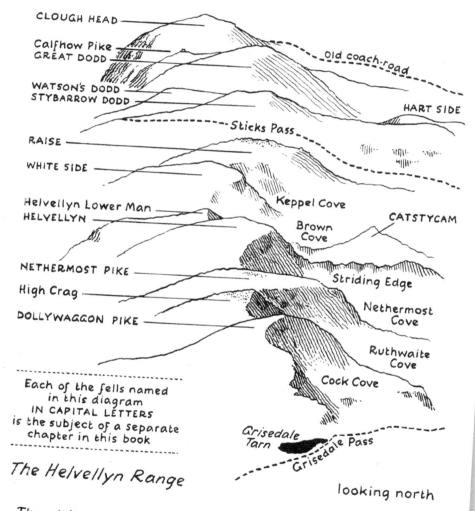

CLOUGH HEAD
Calfhow Pike
GREAT DODD
Old coach-road
WATSON'S DODD
STYBARROW DODD
HART SIDE
Sticks Pass
RAISE
WHITE SIDE
Helvellyn Lower Man
HELVELLYN
Keppel Cove
CATSTYCAM
Brown Cove
NETHERMOST PIKE
Striding Edge
High Crag
Nethermost Cove
DOLLYWAGGON PIKE
Ruthwaite Cove
Cock Cove

Each of the fells named
in this diagram
IN CAPITAL LETTERS
is the subject of a separate
chapter in this book

Grisedale Tarn
Grisedale Pass

The Helvellyn Range

looking north

The altitude of these fells and the main connecting ridges is consistently above 2500 feet from Dollywaggon Pike (2810') to Great Dodd (2807') except for the depression of Sticks Pass, which is slightly below. This is the greatest area of high fells in Lakeland, and the traverse of the complete range from south to north (the better way) is a challenge to all active walkers. (As a preliminary canter, strong men will include the Fairfield group, starting at Kirkstone Pass and reaching Grisedale Tarn over the tops of Red Screes, Little Hart Crag, Dove Crag, Hart Crag and Fairfield)

Views from the mountainside

From the start, he is also opinionated, which adds pleasure to otherwise dry directions when in skilled hands. The very first path outlined, up the 1,424-foot Arnison Crag from Ullswater, berates the starting point of Mill Moss as 'once a pleasant tarn, now a rubbish tip' and describes the ascent as only beginning properly 'after picking a way through the foothills of old tin cans and motor tyres which are much in evidence here'. Likewise he draws an Army firing range's Keep Out notice on the 1,760-foot summit of Great Mell Fell only so that he can nudge readers into ignoring it, with the brief rider: 'Beware flying ammunition of course.' It was early days for a fledgling writer to be exercising the muscle obtained by getting your views into print, but Wainwright clearly enjoys the chance to do just that.

As he roves the eastern patch, he also records many phenomena which have since become better known. On the long haul up 2,350-foot Birkhouse Moor, Book One notes erosion caused by walkers' boots, which even back in the early 1950s had trodden away the earth and left the underlying stones loose. A typical piece of Wainwriting advises that 'pedestrians whose limbs are beginning to creak would be better advised to plod dully up by Mires Beck...' Although full of delight in the beauty of the fells, Book One already has a frank and unsentimental side which further distinguishes the guides: their author calls a dreary walk just that. Of humble Birks, the 2,040-foot spur of shapely St Sunday Crag, he says: 'Being

Keswick and Derwentwater from Blencathra

an unromantic and uninteresting fell, it has earned for itself nothing better than the prosaic and unassuming title of Birks.' The dismissal is reinforced at the top where we learn that 'The summit has no interesting features.' Even the nearby, lower and otherwise undistinguished 1,702-foot fell of Hartsop Dodd had a brief moment of glory as Wainwright records: it made national headlines in 1948 when two hunting dogs fell down a hole and caused an enormous rescue operation.

Across the valley, by contrast, the beautiful 2,917-foot outlier of Helvellyn, Catstycam or Catchedicam, is praised unstintingly as having 'nearly the perfect mountain form' with precipices dropping steeply from its sharply pointed cone, linked to Helvellyn by Swirrel Edge which some judge to be finer than Striding Edge on the other side of Red Tarn. Wainwright now shows his powers of précis as he picks his way down the side of Catstycam to an old miners' aqueduct which snakes round the 1,700-foot contour, cantilevered from sheer rock faces where these lie in its path. 'Student civil engineers may find the old water cut of some interest as it crosses the north face below the crags,' he writes. 'Now disused and unusable, it has become a home for frogs. Firewood is available here in plenty for fell campers.' Now that the remains are preserved, the last tip does not apply, but a fine and varied stash of information is packed into his two sentences.

The discipline of the format required this. The sub-division of each mountain into six sections – natural features, map, ascents, summit, view, ridge routes – leaves limited room for diversions. But as he goes along, he becomes adept at squeezing in comments; where an interesting name arises, for example. He notes on the way up the 2,381 feet of Clough Head above the River Glenderamackin that Fisher's Wife's Rake leads straight to Jim's Fold, and speculates on why a wife should beat so determined a path to Jim. And there are regular pages or half-pages where he allows himself the luxury of a larger-scale drawing of a rock formation, view or object of interest. In Book One he carefully portrays the challenging rock step on the only way up the modest 1,657 feet of Low Pike, adding wryly: 'It is unusual for a distinct track to have so formidable an obstacle but the step is not difficult to climb if the right foot is used first, the right foot in this case being the left. There is no dignity in the proceeding, either up or down.'

Towards the end of the debut volume, playfulness breaks through more often, a final trend which grows as the series develops. After several pages of precise directions on Red Screes, 2,541 feet of complicated cliff and rock formations, Wainwright's imagination takes wing. He invents a table of nine distinctions of the mountain with the warning that some are reliable, others not. They include (unreliably) the claim that tarns near the summit house 'the highest resident tadpole population east of the Keswick-Windermere road' and the fact (unquestionable) that Red Screes alone 'offers alcoholic beverages at 1,480ft'. It does, at the Kirkstone Pass Inn.

Book One is dedicated to the staff of the Ordnance Survey to honour their newly published two-and-a-half-inch to the mile maps of the Lakes – although the tribute does not exempt them from criticism when they go wrong. After chiding the cairn builders on Great Dodd for building below the summit, where there are no stones but only grass, he moves on to Stybarrow Dodd and half a page of maths, inserted on the grounds that the top is so dull that some sums will wile away the bored visitor's time. The result is a reproof of the OS for showing a contour line going up to 2,825 feet when the real height is '2,770ft approx'. The 'approx' is the only one in the series and a tribute to Wainwright's Borough Treasurer mind.

Preceding pages: Tarn on Hardknott, with Ulpha Fell behind. Above: Grains Gill ravine

But now the Eastern Fells were recorded, and the handwritten Personal Notes in Conclusion — another unfailing part of the books' structure — admits: 'Recently my gaze has been wandering more and more from the path and away to the fells east of Kirkstone — my next area of exploration. When this last sentence is written Book One will be finished and in the same moment Book Two will take its place in my thoughts.'

Book Two is *The Far Eastern Fells* and it covers more mountains than any of the other volumes in the *Pictorial Guides*, 36, while describing one of the Lake District's most straightforward pieces of high ground. North and south marches the great flat spine of High Street, the giant of Book Two, with its foothills falling gracefully westwards to the shores of Ullswater and east to the reservoir lake of Haweswater and the final ridges above Long Sleddale, Mosedale and Swindale which lead to the limestone plateau between the Lakeland mountains and the North Pennines. High Street's urban-sounding name is appropriate for the eight-mile summit ridge, wild and consistently over 2,000 feet but a highway for centuries. A Roman road between forts at Ambleside and Brougham ran the length

Kewick and Derwentwater from the slopes of Skiddaw

of the range and its stones are still criss-crossed by walkers exploring the massif. In Wainwright's own words, the fell has been 'known and trodden, down the ages, by a miscellany of travellers on an odd variety of missions; by marching soldiers, marauding brigands, carousing shepherds, officials of the Governments, and now by modern hikers. Its summit has been in turn a highway and a sports arena and a racecourse, as well as, as it is today, a grazing ground for sheep.'

The book exults in the skill of the Romans, whose highway snakes between the ridge's summits, dropping dramatically to the narrow Straits of Riggindale where England's only Golden Eagle roosts, and always with views on every side for watchful legionaries on the march. Wainwright also distributes superlatives generously. He calls the lakeside path by Ullswater below Place Fell without qualification 'the most beautiful and rewarding walk in Lakeland'. Small Water in its cove on Harter Fell is likewise 'the finest tarn in Lakeland – and how the larks sing at dawn on Harter Fell on a summer's day.' The word 'Heavenly' remains a firm favourite.

Yew Tree Farm near Coniston

But he balances such lyrical passages with a clear-eyed acknowledgement of the way that many of his readers are likely to view some of the less-frequented fells. The top of 1,718-foot Bonscale Pike is 'nothing other than a dreary plateau of grass' while 2,339-foot Branstree is condemned as 'a dreary fell which must disappoint all who climb it. By any standards and by any route, the climbing on this flank is completely uninteresting.' The poor 1,585-foot Sour Hows gets the ultimate slap to add to its off-putting name: 'Few other than conscientious guidebook writers will visit its summit.'

This waspish side to the guides began in

Book One, is thoroughly established in Book Two, and becomes one of the series' paradoxical attractions. You can trust a writer who does not flinch from describing the hellish as well as the heavenly. Book Two also gives increasing rein to Wainwright's whimsies. On a windy day atop Grey Crag's 2,286-foot plateau, he describes the racing clouds and streaks of blue sky as 'worthy of the brush of a Turner', but adds: 'The desolation is profound. Solitary walkers who want a decent burial should bear in mind that if an accident befalls them in this wilderness their bones are likely to adorn the scene until they rot and disintegrate.' Waiving his relish

for trespassing for once, he urges walkers three times not to invade the deer sanctuary around the 1,887-foot The Nab, while admitting, below two drawings of a heavily-antlered red deer: 'Some 50 years ago the author carried out his explorations surreptitiously and without permission; he was not detected but this may possibly have been due to his marked resemblance to an old stag. Others should not expect the same good fortune.'

The book's wide range of walks, from the steep haul up Kidsty Pike to the Gatescarth route on 2,552-foot Harter Fell which Wainwright calls 'a hands-in-pockets stroll eminently suitable for nonagenarians', leads readers to many more of the fells' curiosities which only such detailed explorations as his seek out. He squeezes his 6-foot, 14-stone bulk into the crude travellers' shelters at Small Water, concluding that 'once the body is insinuated snugly in their spider-infested recesses, the weather may be defied.' Leaving 2,201-foot Loadpot Hill he reflects on not only its Stone Age ruins but also the fact that, thanks to an abandoned keeper's cottage, 'no other Lakeland fell has a concrete living room floor and the remains of a domestic chimney stack almost on its summit.'

Above: Haystacks. Overleaf: Crummock Water

The cairns of the Far Eastern fells also remained for ever in his and readers' memories, an extraordinary range from the slender 14-foot column on 2,569-foot Thornthwaite Crag to the unique flagpole, now gone, at 2,283 feet on Rest Dodd and a curious arrangement of old iron fenceposts stuck into stone piles on top of Harter Fell, which he illustrates for their 'spectral weirdness and nightmarish quality'. Few things make Wainwright as angry as walkers who desecrate cairns instead of adding the traditional stone of their own to keep the landmarks in good repair as vital waymarkers in mist. One of the few, however, is Manchester Corporation's waterworks, introduced as a dark force in Book Two for turning Haweswater into a reservoir, drowning the Dun Cow at Mardale Head along with the rest of the hamlet, eyeing other valleys in the area, and forcing sparkling becks into 'captive routes to the taps of Manchester'. In his Personal Notes in Conclusion, Wainwright has a very rare moment of self-doubt about this, admitting: 'Perhaps I have been a little unkind to Manchester Corporation... but man works with such clumsy hands.' He returns to belabour the city with relish in later volumes.

And then it was time to go. It was autumn 1956, the series was precisely on schedule and Book Three demanded a move to the busy valley of Great Langdale and the heart of the Lake District. Thanking readers for the offers of help, transport and company which had flooded in after the success of Book One, Wainwright

reasserted his determination to go it alone. 'I am stubbornly resolved that this must be a single-handed effort.' The attitude chimed with the solitary pleasure he took in the vast, quiet emptiness of the High Street range. 'Rarely did I meet anyone; usually I walked from morning till dusk without a sight of human beings. I leave this area to renew acquaintance with the more popular and frequented heights in the middle of Lakeland. I shall enjoy it but it is a weakness of mine to be forever looking back and often I shall reflect on the haunting loneliness of High Street and the sup'eme loveliness of Ullswater.'

Book Three on *The Central Fells* was diaried in for late 1956 to mid 1958 and it took Wainwright into an area of contrasts.

Once again, his slice of the Lakes made good sense, embracing a third almost entirely self-contained massif which runs north and south between Keswick and Grasmere. Much of it is a whale-like mound of high ground whose summits are little more than grassy heaps amid a boggy plateau, but the southern tip breaks out into spectacular crags, precipitous cliffs and the Lake District's most arresting and exciting mountain profile, the spiky skyline of the three Langdale Pikes. Here was Lakeland's signature of huge variety in a modest area in miniature as Wainwright acknowledges in his Introduction: 'a concentration of mountains crowded into small space that for popular appeal and scenic attractiveness ranks second to none'.

Here too comes his first piece of real daring, much the most exciting adventure for readers so far: the ascent of a ledge called Jack's Rake which clings to the vertical south-east face of 2,288-foot Pavey Ark. Lethal drops onto scree far below leave many would-be scramblers completely unnerved, including myself. But Wainwright, although big, often clumsy and prone to duck out of other routes graded as 'easy' rock climbs, wanted this particular prize. He describes how 'for much of the way the body is propelled forward by a series of convulsions unrelated to normal walking,' warns deadpan that 'care should be taken to avoid falling down the precipice' and explains that his excellent sketches of the terrifyingly narrow ledge were done from the Rake's Easy Terrace – 'the only section where the author's mind was not occupied with a primitive desire for survival'. A very fine diagram of the route which takes up a full page helped to seal the series' reputation as a matchlessly comprehensive guide.

Like Book Two, *The Central Fells* puts Wainwright's praise of highlights such as Jack's Rake in the context of a witty jeremiad of complaints about the vast, soggy range to the north of the Langdale Pikes, whose miseries make outstanding armchair reading. Obliged to chart them all, Wainwright trudges in fury over morasses such as 1,570-foot Armboth Fell, 'a waste of time and precious energy', before clambering another 1,665 feet to announce: 'It is hard to imagine that anybody feels any affection at all for High Tove.' The fir plantations around Thirlmere reservoir renew his contempt for Manchester, which he eases only by hints that walkers should enjoy defying 'the No Trespassing notices that the Corporation has sprinkled about'. Those have largely gone in these more enlightened times, as revised editions of the books make clear, but the morasses on the plateau and its dripping valleys are very much still there. Wainwright's recommendation of 'thigh-high gumboots' on the route between Armboth Fell and Ullscarf

holds good and so does his description of a swamp in the Wythburn valley which is so glutinous that the Ordnance Survey actually marks it as The Bog. He writes: 'The Bog (with a capital T & B deservedly) is the official name of this morass. It may be said that here, at any rate, the foot of man has never trod (if it has, it must have made a terrible squelching sound). The valley, besides being a study in desolation (especially in rain and mist) has many geological and geographical features of unusual interest but one visit will be enough for most folk, for the ground is abominably and inescapably WET.'

Such passages sit beside useful practical advice, such as the rule that light-coloured grass indicates firm ground while red varieties, rushes and moss mark thigh-high gumboot traps. Once off the whaleback, Book Three is also as rich as its predecessors in uncovering secret pleasures. By the 1,776-foot summit of Blea Rigg lies a rock pool overlooked by most visitors and, a little lower down, an invaluable rough shelter for use in foul weather. The modesty of Little Grange Fell with its jaunty summit of Jopplety How at 1,363 feet is deceptive. 'It is nothing on the map,' writes Wainwright, 'everything when beneath one's feet. The climb from Borrowdale in autumn is a golden ladder to Heaven. Sacrifice any other walk if need be, but not this.' Bold conquerors of Jack's Rake are advised how to manage the last, desperate haul up the rock summit nicknamed The Howitzer, which tops the 1,328-foot Helm Crag, although Wainwright himself had not succeded. A small box surrounded with a dotted line says in his neat writing: 'This corner was reserved for an announcement that the author had surmounted the highest point. Up to the time of going to press, however, such an announcement cannot be made.' It never was.

Once again, however, he catches out the Ordnance Survey, indulging this little hobby with a note celebrating 'the rare triumph of

Summit of Castle Crag, with Borrowdale valley below

detecting an obvious error on an OS map'. It was only a misprint putting the 1,500-foot contour on Moss Moor as 1,800 feet but that sort of thing made Wainwright's day. The recent wrecking of a cairn at Nab Crags on 2,370-foot Ullscarf also allowed him to flex his growing author's muscle more vigorously than ever. Two teachers who allowed their school party to do the vandalism are called criminal and 'brainless idiots'. Finally, he left Book Three with a rarity, a large-scale drawing of himself, albeit mostly from the side and back, to fill a space left on the page allocated for The View from 1,520-foot Raven Crag. Because Manchester's firs blocked so much of the horizon, the view indicator is unusually small, leaving room 'as a special treat for readers, for a picture of the author apparently contemplating the view (but more likely merely wondering if it's time to be eating his sandwiches)'.

Sprinkling Tarn

Book Four on *The Southern Fells* had been eagerly awaited, well before Wainwright revealed in his Personal Notes in Conclusion to *The Central Fells* that he was now 'hastening to the Scafells, noblest of Lakeland's cathedrals'. The highest land in England was the subject of the new volume, published according to plan in 1960 after an almost miraculously benign season of calm, sunlit weather helping research among the rock walls and complicated ridges of the Scafell and Bowfell massif, the unique magnetic rock of Crinkle Crags and the lower but still challenging Coniston Fells. Here was another division which followed the natural lie of the mountains, with a minimum of links to other fells which walkers might want to take in on a day's walk. Book Four is sufficient on its own for anyone exploring this magnificent area, much of which lies above 3,000 feet.

Longer than all the other volumes, at more than 300 pages, it devotes a record 30 to the crowning heights of 3,210-foot Scafell Pike even though the exhilarating route descriptions are matched by constant references to the tourist hordes and the lack of peace and quiet for solitary souls such as the author. But the real drama lies on the ridge from the Pike to the subsidiary but more precipitous 3,162-foot summit of Scafell, taken all those years ago by Samuel Taylor Coleridge but blocked for Wainwright by the terrors of Broad

Ill Crag

Valley stream

Stand. He sketches an imaginary noticeboard on top of the treacherously slanting rock saying in capital letters: 'Not for walkers'. Squeeze into the cleft at the base known as Fat Man's Agony, he says, but leave it at that. 'For mere pedestrians this is the limit of their exploration and they should return through the cleft, resolving as is customary to do the climb next time. The author first made this resolve in 1930 and has repeated it a score of times since then; his continuing disappointment is amply compensated by the pleasure of going on living. You have been warned!'

As he goes on to explain, the safe alternative route to Scafell is itself an airy and exciting traverse across an exposed rock face, the ledge called Lord's Rake, where the need for most people to slither along one section on their bottoms is compensated for by close-quarters views of the rare starry saxifrage plant. As the book roams the high ground across to 2,960-foot Bowfell and its beetling Great Slab, there are many other fine paths and rock faces – and another cul-de-sac. In Cust's Gulley on 2,984-foot Great End, Wainwright admits 'twice timorously attempting to climb the difficult pitch beneath a huge, edged boulder, before retiring with a jeering conscience to go home and write in capital letters (again): No way for walkers.'

Scafell Pike – the summit conquered. Overleaf: Dale Head summit cairn

The loneliness of the southern approach to the Scafell massif, from Eskdale, brings out the series' love of Lakeland's quiet places with particular force, especially in contrast to Langdale, Borrowdale and Wasdale Head, which are the launch pads for most assaults on Scafell Pike. In the same way, Wainwright hymns the virtues of Wetherlam in the Coniston range, where the majority of walkers make for neighbouring Coniston Old Man. The paramount feature of both these fells in the book, however, is the mark left by man in tunnels, shafts and piles of spoil from 18th- and 19th-century mines. Among many references, Wainwright makes one which reminds us sharply of the private desolation of an author so joyful on the hills. 'These ugly black holes are not merely dangerous but damned dangerous,' he writes of the mines. 'Sons should think of their mothers and turn away. Husbands should think of their wives, after which gloomy contemplation many no doubt will march to their possible doom.'

Stubborn in a different way, Wainwright now turns his eyes north for Book Five, *The Northern Fells*, ignoring pleas and even several petitions from readers that the mighty western neighbours of the Scafells – Great Gable, Pillar and Steeple – should come next. 'What a frightfully untidy suggestion!' he writes in the Personal Notes in Conclusion to Book Four. 'It springs from a generally accepted view, of course, that there is nothing "back o' Skidda"

worth exploring. I want to go and find out.' So between 1960 and 1962 his tall, stolid figure was to be glimpsed (before dodging shyly for cover) on Skiddaw, England's fourth-highest mountain, and its 23 companions. These are geologically Lakeland's oldest hills and form yet another self-contained group: a circle divided between Skiddaw and Blencathra in the south and the Caldbeck and Uldale fells to the north.

In Victorian days the gentle, grassy slopes of Skiddaw were often conquered comfortably on ponies or by a five-mile ride from Keswick in a horse-drawn carriage. The route has even been done by car, and Wainwright's own description starts with the prosaic advice that 'If the railway station is open, there is an unauthorised short cut through the subway.' But his full description of the mountain and seven different ascents to its summit justifies his whimsical thought at one stage that if you asked one of the mountain's sheep what it thought of Skiddaw, 'it would reply "C'est magnifique" (if it was French, which is unlikely).' The 28 pages, only two fewer than the allocation given to Scafell Pike, are one of the most thorough examples of Wainwright's skill at showing how hills which many walkers take for granted are full of surprises, caves, memorials, waterfalls, as well as the opportunity for endless variations of traditional routes.

The A66, gateway to the Northern Lakes, approaching Blencathra

To the east, across Skiddaw Little Man and Lonscale Fell for the very energetic, lies the second giant of Book Five whose attractions are much more obvious. Wainwright set a record with his 30 pages for Scafell Pike; now he breaks it, with 36 for the wonderful mountain of Blencathra. Also known as Saddleback (a name Wainwright disliked as ordinary and shared by other undulating hills), the 2,847-foot peak is introduced as 'one of the grandest objects in Lakeland'. Its greatest glory is the face torn by four ravines which tumble almost vertically down to the Penrith-Keswick road, divided by narrow ridges including the saw-toothed challenge of Sharp Edge. One of the great scrambles in the *Pictorial Guides*, this is described by Wainwright as 'a rising crest of naked rock of sensational and spectacular appearance, a breaking wave carved in stone. The crest itself is sharp enough for shaving (the former name was Razor Edge) and can be traversed à cheval' – Book Five clearly found Wainwright in French mode – 'only at some risk of damage to tender parts. One awkward place calls for a shuffle off a sloping slab onto a knife edge; countless posteriors have

Views of Blencathra

imparted a high polish to this part.'

Away to the north, the other side of the writer emerges as the grandeur of Skiddaw and thrills of Sharp Edge give way to broad and largely featureless fells like Mungrisdale Common — 'back o' Skidda' indeed and dismissed as 'a dreary appendage to the fine mountain of Blencathra'. Wainwright saw only three people here during months of roaming, making him feel that 'I was preparing a book which would have no readers at all, a script that would have no players and no public.' But at the very furthest northern point of his travels, he does not regret extending his diamond-shaped hunting ground to Caldbeck, John Peel's old hunting ground, to include the modest 1,466 feet of far, outlying Binsey. The reason is one of the virtues common to such quieter fells: a magnificent view of their grander neighbours, in this case the whole of the Northern range from Skiddaw to Blencathra. Turning round, the walker on the summit of Binsey takes in the majestic sweep of the Solway Firth with the mountains of Scotland blue and purple far beyond. 'What a domain!' writes Wainwright. 'And what a throne to view it from!'

It was now the autumn of 1961 and he was beginning to feel like a climber within sight of the end of Jack's Rake on Pavey Ark. 'Another one finished!' he writes at the end of Book Five, but not with any sense of a burden at having to work through his two remaining sections. Book Six was to cover *The North Western Fells*, and he risked contradicting previous superlatives by heralding it with the statement that he had 'long considered them to be the most delectable of all'. Making a rare reference to politics, on which he had right-wing Conservative views, he adds in the context of the developing crisis between the Soviet Union and the United States: 'Ready Easter 1964, old Kruschev willing.'

The Cuban missiles turned back, the world rolled on and Wainwright's schedule held. The 29 fells between Buttermere and Derwentwater were presented to readers on time, three compact groups of mountains divided by two passes, each conveniently traversed by a road. Wainwright was not at all averse to walkers getting as high as they could by car, or in his case by bus, especially in an area rich in botanical interest which might attract older readers. 'A good walker,' he says reassuringly for anyone wondering if they are cutting corners, 'never tramps a road that has a bus service.' The giants in this group are Grasmoor at 2,791 feet and Eel Crag, 2,749 feet, bulky

A PICTORIAL GUIDE
TO THE

LAKELAND FELLS

being an illustrated account
of a study and exploration
of the mountains in the
English Lake District
by

AWainwright

BOOK SIX

THE

NORTH WESTERN

FELLS

50TH ANNIVERSARY EDITION

rather than dramatic but with fine views, especially of the Scafell massif brooding to the south-east. Wainwright honours the outlook from Grasmoor with another of his rare large drawings of himself, adding the typical detail of a label on his jacket saying 'Harris tweed'. He gives the crown, however, to Eel Crag in the course of a well-organised geography lesson which concludes that 'Streams from the fell flow into two main rivers, from Grasmoor into one, and this is the great test of superiority. Eel Crag is a watershed and Grasmoor is not.'

Derwentwater

The book also explores one of the very few places in the Lakes where the old quarries are still going, the flourishing slateworks at the summit of the Honister Pass which are overlooked by the much-exploited flank of 2,473-foot Dale Head. You can buy a coaster or an entire kitchen work surface in the excellent showroom, which also gives free tea to walkers – ambrosia on a foul day – though few will snub the suggestion of a voluntary gift to the mountain rescue. The mine also offers an underground tour, but Wainwright prefers his own, through the spoil heaps on Dale Head where bright green veins of copper malachite snake across the hacked stones. The book charts two interesting alternatives to traditional ascents of the fell, through abandoned workings up Newlands Beck and via a tottering, abandoned tramway to Rigghead quarries.

Book Six also includes one of the Lake District's most popular mountains, Catbells, which rises only 1,481 feet above the beautiful, island-dotted reaches of Derwentwater, but is the famed home of Mrs Tiggy-winkle, Beatrix Potter's hedgehog who does the laundry for Peter Rabbit and Squirrel Nutkin. Wainwright writes: 'This is a family fell where grandmothers and infants can climb the heights together, a place beloved.' He does not attempt to track down the hedgehog's burrow, a place better

Working farm

left to the different imaginations of countless children, but describes a pleasant zigzag alternative to the main, busy start of the climb at Hawse End: Woodford's Steps, engineered in Victorian times by a local retired magnate called Sir John Woodford. The guide also adopts a distinctly un-Potterish tone of double entendre in its final summary of the joys of Catbells. 'It has a bold "come hither" look that compels one's steps, and no suitor ever returns disappointed. No Keswick holiday is consummated without a visit to Catbells.'

The final pitch: Book Seven, *The Western Fells*. At last, the patient partisans of Great Gable and Pillar, the last with its celebrated

Rock towering above the lonely youth hostel at Black Sail, knew that their guide was less than two years away. For the last time in the making of the series, Wainwright sallied forth into a new area to deal with the two remaining spokes of his Lakeland wheel, the horseshoe round Ennerdale. This was to become another of the longer books, tackling 33 mountains including a core within a whisker of 3,000 feet. But well below them lies its heart: Wainwright's ultimate favourite and the summit where his ashes now risk getting caught in walkers' boots, the rumpled peak of Haystacks.

Haystacks

The giant of the book is Great Gable, looking down on Haystacks from the head of Ennerdale, where it forms the centrepiece of a majestic circle. Although Gable's higher reaches are what Wainwright calls accurately 'a desert of stones', the fell's pyramid shape and bulk draw the eye from all surrounding ridges. Walkers make for it by instinct. 'It casts a spell,' says Book Seven. 'It starts as an honourable adversary and becomes a friend.' Wainwright's only hesitation is an interesting one, which sheds another light on the reasons for the lasting success of his books. Gable's many attractions, he says, including the spiky Napes Needle pillar of rock, the 'Gable Girdle' which contours round the mountain and Moses' Trod, the old slate-miners' route to both the sea and illicit hooch stills, are too obvious and openly displayed. Anyone can find them. 'There are no cavernous recesses, no hidden tarns, no combes, no hanging valleys, no waterfalls, no streams...' These are the glories which he is so adept at discovering and then guiding his readers towards. Another signature of his books.

Innominate Tarn

The final volume is therefore happier and more in Wainwright's element on Gable's neighbouring giant Pillar, where the crevices and chimneys of Pillar Rock, the finest crag in the Lake District, are given the thorough treatment previously accorded to Jack's Rake and Broad Stand. This is another place where 'mere pedestrians' admire at close quarters, but do not under any circumstances venture in Wainwright's world. Warning that the climbing fraternity's definition of 'easy routes' is no one else's, he introduces a new deterrent pay-off line based on the mountain-rescue kit at the foot of the crag: 'Remember the stretcher box.' Further along the ridge above Ennerdale, the shapely spire of Steeple is another highlight of what Wainwright calls 'the sunset area of Lakeland'. That is an apt valedictory phrase, for, just as the sun illuminates these mountains last of all in the Lake District before sinking into the Atlantic, so the writer is on the final stage of his marathon.

Left: Coniston Old Man from Torver Common. Above: Innominate Tarn

The journey has to end on Haystacks, as the mortal remains of Wainwright were to do when his ashes were scattered after his death in 1991. Because of its modest height, he felt unable to include it in his finest half-dozen fells which are listed in the very last Personal Notes in Conclusion at the end of Book Seven: Scafell, Bowfell, Pillar, Great Gable, Blencathra and the Crinkle Crags. But he considered its summit supreme for simple, enchanting loveliness, made all the better for coming as a surprise after the view from below which often finds the heather and rock looking foreboding and black. The eastern approaches to Haystacks, too, were until recently swathed in regimental conifers which Wainwright loathed almost as much as Manchester Corporation. But the summit... 'For a man trying to get a persistent worry out of his mind, the top of Haystacks is a wonderful cure.'

Above: Haystacks summit with High Crag and Crummock Water in the distance.
Facing page: Conclusion to The Western Fells by A. Wainwright.
Overleaf: Kelly Hall Tarn, near Torver, with Coniston Old Man behind

With his disastrous first marriage, long struggle for self-improvement and inability to convey his real feelings except in print, Wainwright was such a man. The Lake District mountains were undoubtedly his cure. 'Always there will be the lonely ridge, the dancing beck, the silent forest,' he wrote at the very end before signing off his masterpiece at Christmas 1965. 'Always there will be the exhilaration of the summits. These are for the seeking and those who seek and find while there is yet time will be blessed in mind and body.' Get your boots on, get your map out (or better still your Wainwright) and get up early. No one who has walked the fells of Lakeland will disagree.

Haystacks and Book Seven were not to be the full stop Wainwright intended, however. In the Personal Notes in Conclusion he revealed that readers had suggested a further volume on 'The Outlying Fells of Lakeland'; up to 60 reasonably sized hills which stand outside his inventive diamond map and beyond the spokes of its wheel. He had rejected this, he said. But within a few years he was going to have to do something which came to him only with the greatest reluctance. He changed his mind. The cause was partly the sheer pressure of demand from his growing band of admirers, which only a saint could resist; but perhaps more, the effects of increasing age and its inevitable concomitant: the giants of Lakeland were soon going to be beyond his reach.

.... So this is farewell to the present series of books.

The fleeting hour of life of those who love the hills is quickly spent, but the hills are eternal. Always there will be the lonely ridge, the dancing beck, the silent forest; always there will be the exhilaration of the summits. These are for the seeking, and those who seek and find while there is yet time will be blessed both in mind and body.

I wish you all many happy days on the fells in the years ahead.

There will be fair winds and foul, days of sun and days of rain. But enjoy them all.

Good walking! And don't forget — watch where you are putting your feet.

AW.

Christmas. 1965.

When the book appeared under precisely the suggested title, *The Outlying Fells of Lakeland*, in 1974, it arrived larded with explanations that pensioners and others unable to reach the major summits were the target audience. Yes, wrote Wainwright grudgingly on the flyleaf, he had to admit that the 56 walks taking in over 100 fells were in part 'a mopping up operation' for the *Pictorial Guides*. After all, they include Walna Scar which is fully 2,035 feet, and the Bannisdale Horseshoe which undulates for 11½ miles. But he repeats his refrain about old age in as many variations as he can muster:

the book is for white-hairs who refuse to send their boots to a jumble sale; for the seer and yellow who can't drag themselves up Gable, but would go mad just sitting in the valley looking at it. It caters for the mildly infirm, those no longer young and readers 'who, like the author, wish that they were fifty years less old'. The dedication is to 'The Old-Timers on the Fells'. Everyone halfway ancient is included in the audience except, as Wainwright notes with his customary dryness, those suffering from rigor mortis, which he describes as 'something to be avoided for as long as possible'.

The book is particularly full of good things because its hoop of mountains, clustered most strongly in the south of Lakeland but with five outriders up north between Cockermouth and Penrith, are classic Wainwright territory. Many of them were seldom visited before he went off prospecting for routes. Anyone frustrated by the march of organised parties up Rossett Gill or around Stickle Tarn can rejoice in discovering Humphrey Head, Top o' Selside or Caw. The book sets a newly leisurely pace which is also refreshing, and Wainwright's Introduction makes the sound point that 'a summit cairn at 1000ft can be just as exciting as one at 3000. As much can be explored in one mile as in five.' It was good to loll on grassy banks which the author in his twenties would have toiled puritanically past. How nice to find a tearoom at the end of the stroll.

The wry tone continues as Wainwright potters up fells such as the 834-foot Reston Scar, a small but sharply edged hill a mile from the village of Staveley on the main trippers' route from the M6 motorway to Windermere, which he admits having passed for donkey's years and seldom given a second glance. Now it has become a worthy destination, 'a fine place for a siesta with a tarn to paddle in, while the rest of the family go on to Helvellyn'. The gentle amble gives room for more observations than usual and *The Outlying Fells* has considerably

more text in proportion to maps and drawings than its predecessors. It gives the elderly hiker something to read during the many recommended rest halts. There is the tarn on Newton Fell which is said to hide the wreck of the first iron ship ever built; a summit tower on Hampsfell painted with grumpy, eccentric poetry by a Victorian artist; sea cliffs on the northern shore of Morecambe Bay, and even a solitary tree at the foot of Finsthswaite Heights on which 'some young idiot has carved the word "Anarchy".' Wainwright, who held very right-wing views all his adult life, comments tartly: 'He'll learn.'

The completion of the book marked the start of a period which Wainwright's biographer Hunter Davies aptly describes in a chapter heading as 'Books Galore'. Now a well-known name whose style and views were sought after, Wainwright spent his ample retirement time producing collections of drawings, sketchbooks with notes on mountain territory as far away as Wales and the Hebrides, historical tracts about Westmorland researched by Betty and, in the 1980s and early 1990s, the 'coffee table books' with partly recycled text which accompanies beautiful photos by Derry Brabbs. Throughout, the *Pictorial Guides* continued to sell by the tens of thousands annually, and gradually adopted the mantle of a Great Work.

Preceding pages: Autumn from Surprise View. Above: Scafell Pike summit, with Wastwater below.

This led to an interesting coda to the Wainwright Saga, which had its origins when Chris Jesty, a diffident taxi driver who had once worked as a cartographer for the Ordnance Survey, dared to raise a subject in 1980 with Wainwright which had been on many others' minds. Jesty had first contacted the writer seven years earlier, when he was one of many would-be writers and illustrators who sent their material for comment, and usually received generous if plain-spoken advice and help with publishing contacts if AW felt that their work had merit. Jesty's contribution was a neat and accurate panorama from the summit of Snowdon which greatly impressed Wainwright, and led to a flourishing correspondence; not just because of Jesty's skill but thanks to the fact that in several ways, including personal shyness and a devotion to accurate detail, the men were alike. As usual, the 17 years of contact were almost entirely impersonal apart from one brief meeting, but Jesty was greatly encouraged. Even Wainwright's implacable bluntness – which led to a mark of 5/10 for Jesty's first tentative foray into publishing, *A Guide to the Isle of Purbeck*, and the dismissive

Above: Scafell Pike summit. Overleaf: Great Langdale, with the Langdale Pikes behind

comment that 'I haven't read the text, having no wish to visit the Isle' — failed to put him off.

In 1980 he asked the big question: might he be permitted to update the *Pictorial Guides*? He was spokesman for thousands who had remained silent. Scores, possibly hundreds of minor details in the series were by now wrong, and there was an increasing number of larger errors. I remember once following a Wainwright path up Coniston Old Man which he recommended for the sweet display of wild flowers in Spring. I would have needed wings to complete the route, for a reactivated quarry

had eaten the hillside away. No matter, was Wainwright's view during the years he toiled at the guides. He regarded obsolescence as inevitable and acknowledged in his Personal Notes in Conclusion that the guides would have their day eventually, and follow predecessors such as Baddeley into honourable retirement.

By 1980 his attitude was, perhaps naturally, a little grander. Such tampering should not take place before his death, he told Jesty, and this might well not happen for another 20 years (by which time he would have been 102).

Above: The Borrowdale valley. Above right: Seathwaite, Borrowdale, with Great End in the distance

During such a span Jesty's own revisions might themselves require revising, he added tartly. It was a view which appears to have influenced the *Pictorial Guides'* publishers, Michael Joseph, who took over from the *Westmorland Gazette* in 1992. This was not a money-driven battle for control; both the newspaper and the publishing house were part of the conglomerate Pearson Longman which also owned, through Penguin Books, the publishing house of Frederick Warne which continued to make a fortune from the unaltered animal tales of Beatrix Potter.

Wainwright was not – yet – in the Potter league, but his work was treated in the same way. It was ample, beautiful and popular. If it ain't broke, don't mend it.

Jesty didn't give up, however, and Wainwright's undisguised admiration for his work led to Michael Joseph commissioning him to draw some maps for two of the Derry Brabbs books, a task beyond Wainwright's eyesight in the late 1980s. Several years later, the increasing numbers of people using the Pennine Way and the Coast to Coast Walk meant that revision to

Wainwright's guides became pressing to avoid right-of-way and erosion problems which might have led to legal action. Jesty was chosen for the work, but that was it. The *Pictorial Guides* in their unaltered form had become a Grail, and Wainwright's death in 1991, far from releasing the hold on the 'pure', untampered text, only increased the tightness of its grip.

A long way away from the Lakes, however, an unrelated development in publishing was to lead to change. In 1975 a young Oxford graduate in a flamboyant red and black skirt had led a successful strike against 40 redundancies proposed at Collier Macmillan. She was one of their star executive recruits, and the calm but firm way in which she handled negotiations earned her a series of increasingly important promotions. Moving from firm to firm, she set up her own company in her own name, Frances Lincoln, in 1977. She was one of the most admired independent publishers in the country, but the promise of still greater things was robbed in 2001 when she died of pneumonia at the age of only 55.

Robin Hood's Seat

Frances Lincoln's father had been brought up at Appleby in Westmorland, and her husband John Nicoll, who took over direction of the firm on her death, was very much a Lake District man. The son of a shoe company executive who worked in Kendal, he grew up in Kentmere and later inherited his parents' house, spending much happy time there with Frances and their three children. In late 2002 he was therefore electrified when one of his sisters phoned him and asked: 'Have you seen what's in the papers? Can you believe it? Couldn't Frances Lincoln do something?' Nicoll had given up taking a daily newspaper some years earlier, a policy which he has never regretted in terms of taking a calm and balanced attitude to life, but on this occasion he was grateful that someone else was keeping an eye on current affairs.

The news in question was that Michael Joseph had announced it was discontinuing

publication of Wainwright's *Pictorial Guides*. Growing inaccuracy, and the effects of the 2001 foot-and-mouth outbreak (when the Lake District was closed to walkers and the books' sales plummeted) lay behind the decision, along perhaps with a simple failure of imagination. Publishers can sometimes be so focused on the next sensation that an old warhorse in their stable may be underestimated, especially if it needs fettling. That evening, Nicoll had tickets for a concert at the Barbican in London and by chance ran into Helen Fraser, the managing director of Penguin, at the event. The story was true, she confirmed and, knowing that Frances Lincoln specialised in high-quality publishing with many wildlife and landscape titles to its credit, she passed on details of Jenny Dereham, who had been Wainwright's editor at Michael Joseph and was now handling expressions of interest in taking the books on.

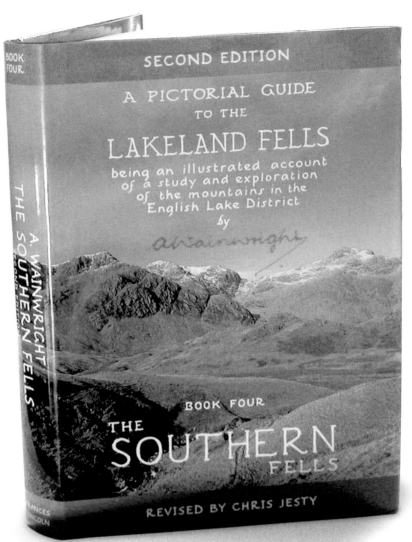

Nicoll had been pondering new directions for Frances Lincoln at the time, and he had a personal enthusiasm for this particular one. He recalls: 'I was a boy when the first Wainwrights came out. My mother bought one and pretty much said: out you go and climb some of these fells.' He did and has done ever since. It would be too much to talk of a Lake District Mafia, but Betty Wainwright, her family and Jenny Dereham clearly appreciated Nicoll's lifelong enthusiasm. Nicoll's parents and Betty had friends in common, and Frances Lincoln fell nicely between big conglomerates, who might begin to succumb eventually to Michael Joseph's waning interest, and local

enthusiasts whose resources were too modest. The deal was done in early 2003 just as the last copies of the existing guides were beginning to run out in the shops. And then there was Chris Jesty.

A man with a mission every bit as strong as his hero's, he had been beavering away on correcting the *Pictorial Guides* purely for his own pleasure – or perhaps as much from a sense of duty, where 'pleasure' could be an inappropriate word. 'I have sometimes felt as though a black cloud was hanging over me, because there is so much to do,' he recalls. He had been getting up as early as 2am to scour the fellsides for changes, sticking meticulously

The ravine on the approach to Great End

to the Master's way of doing things, and he then recorded them at home, down to reproducing Indian-ink Wainwriting in his own neat hand. With the arrival of Frances Lincoln he at last had the equivalent of the US Cavalry coming over the horizon. In place of disinterest and Wainwright's blunt comments of a decade earlier, John Nicoll brought nothing but encouragement. 'When I found out that Chris Jesty had been revising away, I thought: "How fantastic!",' he says. 'What a bonus. How amazingly exciting.'

And so in June 2005 a new era began for the famous series, when Jesty's revised Book One appeared under the Frances Lincoln imprint, with a warm introduction from Betty. Apart from red rather than black lines marking each route, it was indistinguishable from the originals in style and design. But that hid a mountain of new work. Jesty had made 3,000 changes to Book One alone, many minute and all hand-drawn. One relatively brief and simple scramble up Clough Head, which takes only a page in the first new volume, has 30 pieces of 'invisible mending', from minor deviations in the route to vanished walls. *The Guardian* described his contribution as 'a labour of love which almost matches the original epic charting of the mountains by Alfred Wainwright'.

The epic continues, with Jesty using graph paper to plot Wainwright's maps against modern tools of the cartographer such as global positioning satellite data. When Book One was finished, he started pencil drawings for Book Two and fieldwork for Book Three, working like his mentor towards a fixed finishing point in 2009. He loves it, really. On the launch of Book One, he admitted shyly in media interviews that he had only taken one weekend off in two years, and that was to appear on the TV quiz show *Fifteen-to-One*.

'I feel I am fulfilling my destiny,' he added. 'I first saw a Wainwright guide in 1964 and ever since then it has been an ambition of mine to revise them. It's a job that fits me absolutely exactly.'

He will probably never be Wainwright's Boswell. Although plain speaking is commendable, Wainwright showed his harsher side in his dismissive comments on the *Guide to the Isle of Purbeck* in 1984: 'The personal notes are poor, not well composed and largely irrelevant, and would have been better omitted.' The old curmudgeon even added: 'You must avoid using the word "so"; it is no substitute for "therefore".' But Jesty has no designs on outwriting or 'improving' on Wainwright. He is the Great Reviser, and his revised editions are a critical success and selling in great numbers. They are part of the gently changing landscape of the Lake District themselves, and one day his story too will deserve to be fully told.

Left: Great Langdale

Wainwright
The Walks

❶ Haystacks

Ascent from Gatescarth
1,550 feet of ascent
1¾ miles

IN THE EARLY 19th century one of the loveliest valleys of the Lake District was home to a famous beauty of English history, Mary Robinson, who was known as the Fair Maid of Buttermere. An innkeeper's daughter, her praises were sung by the Lake Poets, but she was then seduced by a London bigamist and faced months of court cases, national publicity and shame. But not before she had spent some 25 years in a landscape which Alfred Wainwright so often described as 'Heavenly'.

The fair maid's immediate surroundings include a valley wall of shapely pyramid peaks, the High Stile range, which ends with a crumpled piece of mountain ground, a jumble of rocks and heather whose outline from a distance resembles the topknot of a boy who hasn't brushed his hair for weeks. This is Haystacks, the resting place for his ashes chosen by Wainwright and the subject of his own metaphor, coined one day when he stood on its summit and gazed at the towering nearby mountains of Great Gable, Kirk Fell and Pillar. Haystacks, he wrote, was 'like a shaggy and undisciplined terrier in the company of sleek foxhounds'.

This air of unorthodoxy, so like his own, combined with the fell's intriguing maze of hummocks, winding paths and three quiet tarns, made the summit supreme for him, against the whole of Lakeland's formidable competition. If you want to get close to Wainwright – indeed, as he drily wrote himself, if you want to risk a bit of grit in your boot which might be from his ashes, the summit of Haystacks is the place to be.

The walk starts down in Gatescarth at the head of Buttermere, a typical statesman's farm run for generations by the Richardsons, a very well-known family in the Lakes. They have produced a series of notable fell-runners, those super-beings who dash up the mountains and then seem almost to fly down, covering in minutes what takes the average walker hours. The family previously farmed at Watendlath, the exquisite hamlet above Borrowdale which Hugh Walpole used as the home of Judith Paris in the *Herries Chronicles*. A vigorous but ultimately insoluble argument has always raged between Watendlath's three Bed & Breakfast farms over which was supposed to be the feisty heroine's home.

Gatescarth lies in a dramatic amphitheatre with a view of Haystacks' summit ridge which explains how the mountain got its name. Haystacks derives from the Icelandic for high, column-shaped rocks, which look from here as though they could well be hayricks which the farmer has failed to collect after harvest. It is not a giant among peaks at 1,900 feet, and the ascent from the farm via Scarth Gap, the col between the fell and its loftier western neighbour, the 2,443-foot High Crag, covers only one-and-three-quarter miles. Nonetheless, like many Lake District walks, it sets a steep pace on the first stretch, after a gentle start from the farm and car park through the Richardsons' neatly kept fields.

Warnscale Bottom

If you are new to fellwalking, there is a psychological lesson to be learned once the path crosses a dry-stone wall and takes its leave of a second ascent, which heads off left into the wilderness of Warnscale Bottom, dominated by Green Crag and Big Stack, the sheer cliffs on Haystacks' northern flank. Our way rises straight up ahead to the 1100 contour line at Low and High Wax Knots, a col of jumbled boulders which makes a good place for a rest. Many Lakeland ascents have this first stiff section; my wife always recalls her debut as an entirely urban Londoner, enticed for a weekend with an experienced group, nimble women and men with sturdy legs, who shot up the clamber on to Helvellyn from Thirlmere as if it was High Street, Kensington. But she discovered, as everyone does, that height is gained quickly and a sense of progress comes rapidly until, when you gain the ridges, you seem to be walking along an easy highway in the sky. Wainwright held that you should find your own pace and then do your best to stick to it. He was ill-equipped to advise parties because he almost always walked on his own; but the sensible rule is to adopt the speed of the slowest member.

Wax Knotts

If this means children and other energetic walkers feeling frustrated, there are plenty of small diversions to be made on most routes, and this stretch to Scarth Gap is typical. The path climbs clearly and it is safe to stray from it to examine small rock faces, one with a lone rowan tree growing straight out of its crevices, or a waterfall which splashes down above the route shortly after Wax Knotts. Something else may be splashing down. Wainwright took his last major fellwalk up Haystacks and was rained on for most of the journey. 'Haystacks shed tears for me that day,' he wrote afterwards. If you are enveloped in mist and have no one experienced in the party, discretion is better than valour once Wax Knotts have been passed. The path is well cairned as far as Scarth Gap, where it drops easily down into the lonely head of Ennerdale and England's most isolated youth hostel at Black Sail. As for higher up. Wainwright writes drily: 'The only advice that can be given to a novice lost on Haystacks in mist is that he should kneel down and pray for safe deliverance.'

In clear weather, the views behind and below from Wax Knotts are sensational: Buttermere winding away down the valley with its pinched-in waist where the village stands, and beyond it the silver of Crummock Water. Wainwright considered it 'a test of iron discipline' to resist halting here, but let us ignore him for once, albeit briefy. Herdwick sheep crop the bilberries nearby, light and shade play on the valley, and across Warnscale Bottom a distinctive white cross of the face of Fleetwith Pike marks where Fanny Mercer fell to her death in 1887. She was a young girl out on the crags but inexperienced in the use of her alpenstock stick, who slipped and tumbled from a normally safe cescent onto an unforgiving, sharp slate outcrop. The Lake District has many such memorials but the national park has now placed a limit, and new ones are always removed. Wainwright supported this policy and, although he raged against the destruction of important cairns, he was also generally opposed to the building of new ones, comparing them on some routes to road traffic cones.

The path is now approaching Scarth Gap and a change in the landscape from sheep-nibbled grass and fox-coloured bracken in autumn to more stony ground. The journey so far has been what Wainwright summarises as 'a prelude of much merit' and one of the

Haystacks

1900' approx.

properly Hay Stacks (two words) as on Ordnance maps

from Gamlin End, High Crag

From The Western Fells by A. Wainwright

Gatesgarth
HIGH ●
▲ CRAG

HAYSTACKS
▲

Black ●Sail Y.H.
MILES

0   1   2

disadvantages in his day has been eased. There were once well-engineered zigzags on this last stretch to the col, but the sheer number of walkers gradually turned them into a scree of boulders, sometimes ankle-wreckingly loose. Now the national park's skilful path-builders have created a rock stairway and the eroded

fellside has a chance to recover. At the top a grassy saddle spreads out, with Haystacks rising rockily to the left and the steep, straight slope up High Crag leading off to the right. A large cairn stands by this crossroads, handsome enough for Wainwright to mark it with a firm triangle on his map of this ascent.

It may seem a lonely place, but the pass has historically been an important trade route and link between Buttermere and not only Ennerdale, but Wasdale and the Cumbrian coastal ports beyond. It remains a scene of workaday human activity with a new sheep fence, today's successor to the dry-stone wall, running across the col. The name is an instance of linguistic repetition, deriving from the Old Norse 'skard', which means a gap in the hills. It is thus 'Gap Gap' in the same way that Lancashire's Pendle Hill means 'Hill Hill Hill', coming as it does from three linguistic strands, Celtic, Norse and modern English, all describing the same thing.

The route now addresses itself to the summit bastion of Haystacks, bringing a fresh and refreshing change as it scrambles up steeply between heather-covered rocks. The scar of thousands of previous boots and small sections of gravelly path show the way ahead clearly, although, as you gain height, fresh views open up and constantly distract your attention. Beyond the Buttermere valley, the Solway Firth gleams in front of Scotland's mountains, and gradually Ennerdale appears to your right. This is a very special Lake District valley with a happy future after decades of highly controversial forestry which angered many in Lakeland in Wainwright's day. His books repeatedly condemned the soulless planting of regimented conifers here, a dark blanket which crushed the subtle range of colours that had existed for centuries. Now at last, the trees are being cropped. Already the blanket has shrunk from the lower slopes of grand mountains such as Pillar, clearly visible from your perch on Haystacks' summit path. The effect is a tidemark of stumps and debris, but that will soon change. Energised by the return of daylight, Nature is rapidly reclaiming the ground and mankind is helping her. The Wild Ennerdale Partnership, which includes the Forestry Commission, is banning all but emergency traffic from the valley's rough roads. Even Black Sail youth hostel will be reprovisioned on pony or by foot.

Black Sail

Black Sail is tucked below Haystacks and occupies a similar exalted place in the minds of many Lake District enthusiasts. My grandfather used to recite a long poem of rhyming couplets, each on a mountain, valley or lake, which ended triumphantly: 'Black Sail – All Hail!' A converted shepherds' bothy, it looks out on a stupendous panorama of high fells, with a convenient bench dedicated to a Leeds youth worker who introduced thousands of city kids to this special landscape and is justly honoured for so doing. Staying overnight is an experience which sets the most restless mind at ease with the world, provided no one else in the modest bunk area snores.

You may need hands as well as feet towards the crest of the summit path until a final shoulder leads to Haystacks' highest point, marked by a cairn assembled round an iron post. The pastel colours of the different stones left by hikers, many of them in shades of soft grey, some beige and fawn and a few with the mossy green of lichen, reflect the exceptionally varied terrain at the top of the peak. 'This is the best fell-top of all – a place of great charm and fairyland attractiveness,' writes

Wainwright. Who could disagree?

The distinction from rivals lies in the miniature chaos of boulders, cliffs, bosky undergrowth, erratic sheep paths and three lovely tarns. One is in a cleft only feet below the summit, where I once startled a couple in a bivouac by appearing just after dawn, having set out very early on a summer's day from Honister youth hostel, which is already very high up. To add to the shock, I had thought myself alone and was talking absent-mindedly to some sheep.

Innominate Tarn

The finest pool of water lies a little lower, Innominate Tarn where Wainwright's ashes were scattered. Except in rough weather, it is beautifully quiet, with clear water over a pebbly bed and fringed by reeds. Behind stand sentinel the high peaks around Great Gable and on all sides a splendid panorama stretches away. On a weekday, you may also see unexpectedly creeping about in the foreground to the north-east a yellow caterpillar excavator in Dubs quarry above Warnscale Bottom, which has been reopened. I do not think that Wainwright would have objected, in the way that he would certainly have resented a school party tramping chirpily across his favourite refuge. His father was a stonemason and it is perhaps appropriate that others in the craft earn a living not far from the writer's resting place.

First-timers may wish to retrace their steps to Gatescarth, no bad thing because you no longer have to look over your shoulders to enjoy the views of the Fair Maid's vale. Alternatively, an excellent route also described by Wainwright in Book Seven, *The Western Fells*, winds down towards Dubs quarry and then turns for Gatescarth through the shattered chasm of Warnscale.

② Blencathra

Ascent from Scales
2,250 feet of ascent
2¾ miles

ALFRED WAINWRIGHT KNEW Blencathra better than all the rest of his 214 fells, giving it more pages in the bocks than any of the others. He describes 12 main alternative ways to reach the summit, a pert crest on a long whaleback, and suggests many variations in between. The mountain's vast hump runs smoothly west to east and thousands of walkers make the undemanding tramp this way every year. Wainwright doesn't recommend that. His usual minute inspection of the terrain became almost microscopic among the four dramatic combes which are scooped out of the mountain's southern face, each with ridges whose narrowness, in the case of his favourite ascent, Sharp Edge, comes close to the width of a saw blade. This is where he points us, and this is where we are going to go.

Guests of Blencathra, a mountain of special character whose many devotees regard it as an almost animate friend, are entering the Lake District's far north. Their host is a great big hulk of land rising to 2,847 feet which forms the final bastion before the gentler hills leading down to the Solway Firth. Wainwright loved this fell for its size and shape, its evocative name and, as he wrote, 'most of all because it is a mountaineer's mountain'.

He drew this conclusion from a whole winter spent in 1960 on the south face, researching for Book Five, *The Northern Fells*, in which he describes his findings in dramatic terms. The four ravines and the five spurs which divide and enclose them struck him as: 'A scene of devastation, the wreckage of what appears to have been, in ages past, a tremendous convulsion that tore the heart out of the mountain and left the ruins in a state of apparently tottering collapse. The result is chaotic: a great upheaval of ridges and pinnacles springing out of dead wastes of scree and penetrated by choked gullies and ravines, the whole crazily tilted through 2,000 feet of altitude. Even in this area of confusion and disorder, however, Nature has sculpted a distinct pattern.'

We must start climbing to see the scale of this wild debris, which hides in its hanging valleys well above the gentle fields around Scales. But scoping out the foothills from the White Horse pub in the village, the variety of colours on the fellside is immediately striking: green for the shoulders of sheep pasture, brown or emerald in high summer for the bracken, grey, purple and black for the tips of the crags higher up. The start of the walk is therefore a comedown. We have to cross the endlessly busy A66 between Keswick and Penrith, a road which Wainwright abhorred. 'Where are the men of vision in authority?' he demanded, knowing that most of them were colleagues in his own Monday–Friday, nine-to-five working world of local government. 'Fragrant lanes and narrow winding highways add greatly to the charm of the valleys; it is an offence against good taste to sacrifice their character to satisfy speeding motorists and roadside picnickers.'

Mousthwaite Combe

As far as the A66 bypass of villages such as Scales and neighbouring Threlkeld was concerned, Wainwright lost. And, as we start to climb up the base of Blencathra, the rumbles and hums of the traffic are an unwanted companion on the walk. Not until the ridge above Mousthwaite Combe has been reached and the chance taken to drop down the other side, is the noise lost and replaced by the splashing of mountain streams.

The initial slope was dappled with bracken, yellow gorse and mountain trees such as the rowan but, as the path climbs, sheep pasture begins to alternate with straw-coloured, windblown stretches of longer, sour tussocks and, down in the combe, reeds and the red-coloured grass which signals a marsh. A much less distinct path like a spore forms a crossroads, left to the summit of one of Blencathra's daughters, Scales Fell, and right to another, Souther Fell, where a ghostly army of horsemen was seen in 1735. We march straight on, then hairpin to the right and then left before settling above the 1500ft contour on the side of the valley of the Glenderamackin, a river as sweet as its name, which tumbles down to join the Greta near Threlkeld.

Scales Tarn

A sense of excitement grows as the valley narrows and gets wilder, stony outcrops becoming ever more frequent amid the grass. The path crosses a succession of waterfalls, switchbacks every now and then and in places creeps along like a sheep track. There are several of these on the other side of the Glenderamackin, narrow strips of worn-away grass where the sheep process in succession like the carriages of a London Underground train. For contrast, glance back to the main valley, now far behind, and the gentle fields of St John's Vale in front of the Helvellyn range. But thoughts will be turning to the challenge which lies ahead, one of the fiercest for the walker in all seven *Pictorial Guides*: the airy scramble up Sharp Edge.

Dramatically, this comes into view for the first time when the Glenderamackin valley path finally plucks up courage to tackle the 1,600 to 1,800-foot contours and reaches the lower and much gentler foot of the ridge. The jagged fangs of the Edge's skyline look impregnable at first sight, tilting like a petrified wave towards the east. But we have a place to pause to summon up all reserves and it is a pleasant one, by the side of Scales Tarn. Let us hope the weather is holding, always an unpredictable factor in the Lake District and especially when you cross from one valley such as the Glenderamackin's to another like the bowl filled by Scales Tarn.

The mountains form a micro-climate so precise that you can bask in sunshine in the first, but have to run for cover in the next. Particularly if we are to believe Sir Walter Scott.

He came this way and was so struck by the brooding silence of the trapped water, and especially by the ominous silhouette of Sharp Edge above, that he wrote the quatrain:

Never sunbeam could discern
The surface of that sable tarn
In whose black mirror you may spy
The stars while noontide lights the sky

Seldom one to quote poetry in his books, Wainwright couldn't resist this, but only for the pleasure of adding: 'These words are well larded with poetic licence. I have sat in warm sunshine by Scales Tarn, and never have I seen stars reflected on the surface of the water. Of more interest are lava deposits in the vicinity.'

So there. Wainwright would not sit for long by Scales Tarn these days, especially in sunshine, when you are unlikely to have your elevenses or picnic lunch on your own. But company is reassuring before an assault on Sharp Edge, and anyway this is a good place to rest and reflect, for all the world like a speck in an enormous bathtub, gouged out by a long-gone glacier, of which Scales Tarn conceals the plug.

Then onwards, if your nerves are steady. It is of course quite permissible to turn back or to divert to the other bank of the tarn where an easy although unpathed route leads to the broad shoulder of Doddick Fell which runs unadventurously up to Blencathra's summit. One of the heroes of the Wainwright story freely admits to bottling out of Sharp Edge. When Chris Jesty was revising *The Northern Fells*, he came to the foot of the ridge and looked up. Then he climbed Blencathra by an easy route, went to the top of the Edge and looked down. 'If it was me doing it, I'd go a different way,' he decided, concluding correctly that this bit of Wainwright's mapping needed no updating.

The great man had already anticipated this. Writing slightly irritably about readers who accused him of mentioning non-existent walls or posts (which had disappeared since he recorded them), he said: 'Such changes are trivial, merely a plucking of little threads in the tremendous backcloth of the mountain scene and of no consequence in the general pattern. Mickledore will be just the same in a thousand years, Sharp Edge no less sharp.'

Sharp Edge

It is sharp, very. Wainwright's worries about its effect on his and others' tender parts had been anticipated, often, many years before.

A Victorian explorer called Green, for example, left a record of how: 'From walking erect, we were reduced to the necessity either of bestriding the ridge or moving on one of its sides with our hands lying over the top, as a security against falling into the tarn or into a frightful gully, both of immense depth. Sometimes we thought it prudent to return, but this seemed unmanly, and we proceeded, thinking with Shakespeare that "dangers retreat when boldly they're confronted".'

This is the right spirit for Sharp Edge, coupled with practical measures such as making sure you always have three points of contact – feet and hands – on the rock. There is no need to tightrope-walk along the actual crest, although the nerveless may. A narrow path accompanies the ridge on the northern side at just the right height to follow Mr Green's second strategy. The airy section is also a great deal shorter than Striding Edge on Helvellyn, although steeper and higher.

It is impossible to lose your way, which makes mist less of an anxiety than wind or ice and there is only one 'bad step' where you need to lever yourself across a stairway of big, sloping slabs before the final toil up the river of stones on the face of Foule Crag, the tower which ends the ridge. Take it easy, go at your own pace, and on the awkward bit, hold your body away from the rock so that you can see what your feet are doing. Watch your balance too, especially if you have a haversack. But this is not a rock climb and there is never any need to swing your body up and trust to momentum, as on the vertiginous Jack's Rake up Pavey Ark. Then it is all over and the rest is a doddle, lifted for most of us by exultant feelings of triumph against dreadful odds. One curious experience which happened to me long ago may incidentally be yours: I met the Blencathra

foothounds at the bottom of the Edge. Wonderful, long-limbed athletes, they roam tirelessly across the fell and its surroundings with their followers chasing behind on foot, the huntsmen and women dressed in British racing green and many of the rest in the grey of John Peel, whose home was not far beyond the other side of the mountain.

Saddleback

From the top of Foule Crag, the summit ridge of Blencathra stretches uneventfully westwards, unbelievably broad and green after the dizzy clamber required to reach it. A gravelly track marks the way to the highest point, dipping down and up a col which gives the fell its alternative but more ordinary name of Saddleback, which Wainwright would not countenance. His appeal to readers to build a decent cairn at the summit still awaits a response, the trouble being that there are very few big stones nearby. Lakeland awaits a successor to Harold Robinson of Threlkeld, who spent years in the mid-20th century ferrying white quartz-rich stones to lay out the 16 by 10-foot cross laid in a hollow off the route between Foule Crag and Blencathra summit, in memory of a fellwalker who strayed in bad weather and lost his life.

Coleridge declaimed up here:

On stern Blencathra's perilous height
The winds are tyrannous and strong

But more excitement is likely to be got from the view, both nearby if you peer down the shattered south-face precipices, and beyond to Scotland, southern Lakeland, the Pennines, everywhere. Any of Wainwright's 11 alternative routes lies ahead to get you down, and none of them will set your hair on end like Sharp Edge.

③ Castle Crag

Ascent from Grange
700 feet of ascent
1 ½ miles

WHY CLIMB CASTLE Crag, a molehill among fells and the only one in the Wainwright books which fails to reach a thousand feet, which is the generally accepted minimum qualification for a mountain? The answer is clear as soon as this striking natural fortress comes into sight beyond the southern end of Derwentwater, where it forms one steep half of the narrow Jaws of Borrowdale. It has everything a Lake District fellwalker could want, but all in miniature. 'If a visitor to Lakeland has only two or three hours to spare, poor fellow, yet desperately wants to reach a summit and take back an enduring memory of the beauty and atmosphere of the district, let him climb Castle Crag,' says Wainwright. On the other hand, with a handful of children or a dog, a good picnic and a taste for hide-and-seek or kick-the-can, you could happily spend an entire day here, and not want to go home.

The crag is a short climb but with an angle of ascent which can still have you puffing and sweating; it has a sylvan approach along a riverbank, but a workaday history which saw quarrymen use gunpowder to blow much of it to smithereens. From the starting point in the comfortable village of Grange it really does look like a castle, a Disney one whose witches' hat turrets have been replaced by the sloping branches of dark fir trees. The first stretch of the walk follows a meandering lane through trees alive with birdsong in season, delightful even when busy with trippers – and Grange's National Trust car park hosts an average of 200,000 vehicles a year. The landscape here has long been used to visitors and the incursions of mankind. Even in Wainwright's day in the 1960s there were 100 men still employed in quarrying locally and five times as many in the Borrowdale slate mines.

Their history is part of this walk, along with the Herdwick sheep which have browsed the valley intakes since the Vikings introduced them, alongside another, highly unusual way of making a living. Borrowdale was the scene of national excitement in 1550 when Britain's first graphite vein was discovered by a shepherd. The rare material was so valuable for military use in artillery fuses that consignments left the valley only under armed guard. Later it became a staple of the pencil industry which, made the name of Lakeland Pencils in Keswick world-famous.

Relics of mining are everywhere on this walk, in spoil heaps, rock faces blasted sheer from the fellside and especially caves. But before reaching the scarred area, the path dawdles along beside the rippling Derwent whose rapids interrupt a succession of tranquil pools, still as millponds with trout rising to flies and many families of inquisitive ducks.

High Spy

The route's many varieties also take in a crossing of the National Trust campsite, heady with the smell of frying bacon from late breakfasters' tents, before it plunges back into the woods, mixed deciduous and conifers, and curves to the right along the old quarrymen's road. On either side there are fallen trunks, stumps and live trees which all share one thing; a velvety covering of moss. This is the rainiest part of England, with an annual average of 140 inches recorded at Seathwaite. The Langstrath Inn at nearby Stonesthwaite even has a carved slate plaque on the wall saying 'In loving memory of a Sunny Day in Borrowdale'. It doesn't risk giving a date; but don't worry. This is a short walk and there's plenty of shelter. And anyway, the sun does quite often shine here. The track heads gently for the narrow gap

between Castle Crag and the main fellside of High Spy, lovely name, which towers 2,143 feet above. Although so much smaller, Castle Crag's isolation exaggerates its size and steepness and from here it does a fair bit of towering itself, the summit vegetation giving an extra, exotic touch of Sir Arthur Conan Doyle's Venezuelan plateau, the Lost World.

Wainwright was in one of his rather pedantic, long-winded moods when he made some of his descriptions of the castle, describing it at various times as 'an obstruction in the throat of Borrowdale' and 'a protruberance on the breast of Scafell Pike'. Never mind; he would have wanted us to come to our own conclusions, and there is lot more evidence still to gather as the walk starts seriously to head uphill. A gate out of the plantation of Dalt's Wood leads to one of those sudden changes of scenery in which the Lake District specialises; from the green shade of the wood, we are now on to open fellside, with its short grass dotted with yellow tormentil flowers, clumps of bilberries and nibbling sheep. You may well meet a flock on their way to Grange or Rosthwaite in the care of a shepherd, whistling a sequence of thin reedy calls to his dogs. These, like barked orders which have the collies rushing to and fro in precise patterns, are part of an ancient culture which also includes ancient versions of numbering. One to twenty? No, it's yan, tan, tethera, eddera, pip, azar, sezar, akker, conter, dick, yanadick, tanadick, tetheradick, edderadick, bumfit, yanabum, tanabum, tetherabum, edderabum, jigget. Try it on the shepherd, but be warned – there are many local variants.

The valley remains narrow and if anything its walls on either side seem to get closer. A man with a big stick could hold off an army here, thought Wainwright. More practically,

it was a tricky place for him to exercise his amateur camera skills; and there was a lot to photograph here. He never drew while out on his walks; the business of setting up an easel and sorting out pens and ink would have been much too hazard-prone in the open air for his meticulous ways. He took amateur photographs and then stuck them together at home, altering perspectives cleverly where necessary to fit a particular section onto his small, genuinely pocket-size pages. In these recesses, his studies of caves are admirable considering the problems of adequate light and the complicated details of the broken rock.

Millican Dalton

Some are natural but most were made by the quarrymen and miners, probing the hill for seams or sections of rock where the slate or stone would split away. One of the biggest holes in the great crag ahead became the roost for years of a remarkable Lakeland character, the Professor of Adventure, Millican Dalton, one of whose many firm but ambiguous views is still incised above the entrance: 'Don't!! Waste words, jump to conclusions.' Did the 'Don't!!' apply to both, or just to wasting words? Was jumping to conclusions reprehensible or a welcome sign of high spirits? Dalton died in 1947, so we have to decide for ourselves.

Castle Crag

985' approx.

From The North Western Fells by A. Wainwright

He was a London insurance clerk from a Quaker background who opted out of conventional life in the 1880s and came to live in this cave in the summer. When the days grew shorter and colder, he returned south to a den in Epping Forest, sometimes interrupting these migrations by leading snow-climbing parties in the Alps. He was not remotely a burden on society. He earned a good living making haversacks and tents, always recognisable as 'Millicans' because, though adept with a sewing machine, he didn't bother to finish the final seams. He also led what he called 'Lake District camping holidays, mountain rapid shooting, rafting and Hairbreadth Escapes'. He travelled to Keswick occasionally on a home-made raft of extraordinary design (a good photograph of it is sold in the town's shops) and his copy of the Labour-supporting *Daily Herald* waited for him every morning in the Post Office at Rosthwaite. Tall, lean and bearded, he always wore shorts which he insisted he had invented in their baggy Boy Scout form, disputing a rival claim by Lord Baden-Powell. He enjoyed controversy, telling friends about a long dispute he had enjoyed with the Astronomer Royal about the night sky: 'He said I was wrong but I have reason to believe that he was.'

Dalton lived to the age of 80 and you can inspect his old 'Cave Hotel', where he carefully covered a mattress of leaves with down quilts (he did not believe that camping had to be the same as roughing it). An upper cave is still there, which he used as a guestroom for friends who were fed on nuts, dried fruits, wild berries, potatoes and porridge. More than anything else, Dalton was associated by his many acquaintances and clients with impossibly strong coffee. To celebrate his 50th climb up Napes Needle, a slender spire on the side of Great Gable, he built a fire on the tiny summit and heated up a billycan of his mudlike brew. Then he got out his Woodbines and puffed contentedly away until twilight fell.

The curl of woodsmoke which marked Dalton's residence no longer rises above the trees, nor does his trademark question to women novices on his rock-climbing courses: 'Skirt detachable? Take it off.' But his spirit is a good one to keep us company as the path turns left and abruptly up the side of Castle Crag proper. This is the potentially sweaty bit, heading for the main, now disused, quarry which produced stones for the countless local dry-stone walls. These are worth examining for the careful design which lies behind the informal appearance: big stones underpin smaller ones up to a sort of coping, with long ones crossing through the whole wall at intervals to pin it together. The first part of the track accompanies a wall which could well have been built as a showpiece for clients, and is ideal to examine.

William Hamer

The view is at long last opening up, and a thoughtful resting place is provided on a wooden seat beneath a plaque explaining that this was a favourite spot of Sir William Hamer, a London doctor specialising in the study of epidemics, and his wife Lady Agnes. They are worthy of remembrance because they bought Castle Crag and gave it to the National Trust in 1920 so that we could all continue to enjoy it. Sir William was a sprightly neighbour for Millican Dalton to have. Promoting his then unusual speciality at the Royal Society of Medicine, he likened it to Sleeping Beauty, adding that bacteriologists – rivals of epidemic consultants at the time – were the bad fairies who had cast the spell.

Only the last haul lies ahead but it is another steep one. After some grassy hummocks, the route zigzags up a great pile of quarry spoil where blasting went on until the 1960s. At the top are the actual quarries, walls of rock and a hollow which is usually dotted with patterns of odd cairns, piles of rocks each with a tall, spike-shaped one like a shaft. Reminiscent of some sort of pagan festival, these are sometimes removed but have always reappeared. You probably need to come on the night of the full moon to discover what is going on.

Then a final clamber to the grassy summit, torn by one final rent cut by the quarrymen – marked with a plaque in memory of Borrowdale's war dead and, often, wreaths of poppies. Circle above this to a natural viewing platform looking out over Derwentwater. On the other side of the fell is the miniature capital of the upper dale, Rosthwaite, and this place between them is 'the loveliest square mile in Lakeland' according to Wainwright. If for any reason you are feeling a bit cross with him, you can take sneaky pleasure from the fact that this is one of the very few summits whose height he got wrong; it was not on the Ordnance Survey and he calculated from the contours on High Spy that it was 985 feet; in fact, it is only 951. If you are one of his 'poor fellows' who has only two or three hours in the Lake District, you had better now scamper back to Grange. Otherwise, what better place to spend the rest of the day?

④ Scafell Pike

Ascent from Borrowdale via
Esk hause 2,900 feet
5½ miles

ENGLAND'S HIGHEST MOUNTAIN is the ultimate challenge for the Lake District walker, a long hard day rewarded by the triumphant knowledge that, when you stand on the summit amid a desolation of broken rocks, you are higher than everyone else in the country. Higher that is, provided the next or previous person in the queue isn't taller than you are. There is plenty of room on the monster cairn for gawpers at the view, and there are usually plenty of them gawping.

For this reason, Scafell Pike was never a personal favourite of Alfred Wainwright, but he knew his duty and expresses it firmly in the books. 'The ascent of Scafell Pike is the toughest proposition the "collector" of summits is called upon to attempt, and it is the one above all others that, as a patriot, he cannot omit.' So slip your folding Union Jack into the haversack alongside a water bottle and packed lunch and turn your face upwards, putting your best boot forward for a haul of at least seven hours from Seatoller car park in Borrowdale.

Because this is a genuine marathon, it is best for those who have never been before to wait for a good weather forecast and start early. It is ultimately impossible to be sure of steadily clear conditions in these fickle mountains, but a tranquil midsummer spell gives a good chance. There are almost always plenty of people on the mountain and mist is not a serious problem, even on the long, stony summit ridge where the way is marked by the rubs and scratches left by countless boots. But the walk and the unparalleled views from the top are infinitely better when the clouds lift.

Scafell Pike is built on a lavish, spreading scale with outriders which are major mountains in their own right. Short ascents are therefore also steep, notably from the rock climbers' Valhalla of Wasdale Head or the solitary wanderer's favourite of lonely Eskdale. Our approach is lengthy in miles but gentler in gradient. It rises from the valley floor of Borrowdale in a series of huge steps, each like the landings of a giant's house, and there are good things to see at each stage.

Seathwaite Farm

It will be an unusual thing if there are not already cars parked at Seathwaite Farm when you arrive, sort out your picnic and equipment – take a compass and know how to use it in mist – and head past the neat, cream-washed buildings. We can reckon on spending the rest of the day on the fell, there and back, even if the immortal fell-runner Joss Naylor managed to reach the top in 47 minutes. His descent has never been forgotten by those who saw it. A helicopter was tracking him and he used its downdraught to almost literally float down the fell. The runners work on the principle of flying between steps on the descent, each foot touching the ground so fleetingly that its owner is almost permanently airborne. It doesn't always work. One champion finished the annual Grasmere fell race with two broken ankles (and he was still running). But Joss and his helicopter were a dream team.

The path initially heads south beside the river Derwent, now a mountain torrent rather than the broad river which babbles its way into Derwentwater beyond the village of Grange. Wainwright first came this way as an earnest young clerk escaping on holiday from Blackburn Town Hall. He had what he called 'sturdy shoes', one set of clothes and a mac. Nowadays, the lightweight walking stick is all but universal, often used in pairs, and a party of walkers in coloured anoraks resembles nothing so much as an ice-cream van's drinks-on-sticks. Clothing and equipment are a matter of personal choice. Wainwright would have wanted you to be comfortable but also prudent, equipped to meet any change for the worse.

Stockley Bridge

The summit is three miles from Seathwaite Farm as the crow flies, but we are not crows and the path soon starts meandering about, particularly after Stockley Bridge, a lovely packhorse arch which carried the old track between Borrowdale and Wasdale. During the last century it gradually fell into disrepair and a smart and full-scale restoration has come in good time, because the bridge is probably now more frequently crossed than ever before. It marks the junction where hikers either carry on up the narrowing ravine of Grains Gill as we shall do, or turn right along the side of Styhead Gill's cascades to Sty Head tarn, at 1,500 feet an alternative launch pad for the final assault on the Scafell Pike massif.

The bridge and a narrower wooden companion higher up Grains Gill are also essential for crossing the Derwent and its feeder becks in spate, when stepping stones or daring leaps are out of the question and a drenching in the icy water risks exposure. The path now steepens up the side of the gill, whose waterfalls and deep rock pools overhung with rowan are entrancing. Severe erosion here has been skilfully tackled by the stonelayers of the national parks footpath team. Sacks of huge rocks dropped by helicopter are dug into the fellside in a pleasantly uneven pattern, forming a staircase which will last for years. Would Wainwright have approved of what some call 'crazy paving in the sky'? 'Mmmm,' says a pathlayer taxed with this unanswerable question. 'I think he might have tapped his pipe, muttered something inaudible and disappeared.' But the repairs earn little but thanks from the thousands who are tempted here by Wainwright's own descriptions, and they will allow the rest of the overtrampled valley bottom to regenerate.

Scafell Pike 18

ASCENT FROM BORROWDALE
via ESK HAUSE

continued

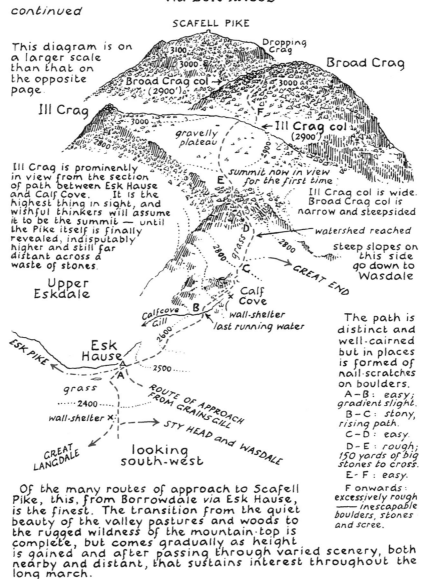

This diagram is on a larger scale than that on the opposite page.

Ill Crag is prominently in view from the section of path between Esk Hause and Calf Cove.   It is the highest thing in sight, and wishful thinkers will assume it to be the summit — until the Pike itself is finally revealed, indisputably higher and still far distant across a waste of stones.

Ill Crag col is wide. Broad Crag col is narrow and steepsided

watershed reached

steep slopes on this side go down to Wasdale

The path is distinct and well-cairned but in places is formed of nail-scratches on boulders.
A–B: *easy; gradient slight.*
B–C: *stony, rising path.*
C–D: *easy.*
D–E: *rough; 150 yards of big stones to cross.*
E–F: *easy.*

F onwards: *excessively rough ——— inescapable boulders, stones and scree.*

Of the many routes of approach to Scafell Pike, this, from Borrowdale via Esk Hause, is the finest. The transition from the quiet beauty of the valley pastures and woods to the rugged wildness of the mountain-top is complete, but comes gradually as height is gained and after passing through varied scenery, both nearby and distant, that sustains interest throughout the long march.

From The Southern Fells by A. Wainwright

Sprinkling Tarn

Looking back, there are now lovely views of Borrowdale and Derwentwater beyond, with little Castle Crag as boldly assertive as ever. Ahead, the path bears left through Ruddy Gill, named after blood-red veins of haematite which also emerge at Ore Gap on Bowfell and turn the surrounding soil a dull maroon. But before plunging onwards, get out the water bottle and a slab of Kendal mint cake and divert briefly on an obvious track to the right. This leads to the beautifully still waters of Sprinkling Tarn, protected by Allen Crags and the lower buttresses of the Scafell Pike range. It is a lonely, special place disturbed only by the sough of the wind through the grass and the harsh cries of ravens which nest in the crags. Often the sense of wilderness is heightened by trails of mist streaming off the precipitous rock wall of Great End, the buttress of the Pike's main ridge. Many walkers miss this spot which is hidden from the Grains Gill path by a gentle mound.

Esk Hause

It is tempting to remain here. Indeed Wainwright evokes the sirens and Circe from the Odyssey, writing: 'The tarn is an enchantress; the temptation to linger is strong, but it must be resisted. "Onwards!" must be the cry. Much remains to be done.' The first task is to hike up Ruddy Gill to the col of Esk Hause, a long diversion around the wall of Great End which no walker can scale. The Hause is the highest walkers' and pony pass in the Lake District, a tilted grassy plateau where four main routes to Scafell Pike from Borrowdale, Eskdale, Great Langdale and Wasdale meet. It was the equivalent of a modern motorway junction in medieval times as pannier-loads of wool were hurried from the valleys to the Cistercian abbey at Furness, whose monks were hard taskmasters and penalised deliveries which came late. The final haul to the Hause is another place where the pathbuilders have freed walkers from the agonies of loose scree created by their impatient predecessors. Wainwright greatly deplored the wrecking of another carefully engineered set of zigzags up this slope, and concluded his condemnation with a memorable aphorism: 'A good walker will climb Scafell Pike and hardly disturb a single stone; a bad walker will leave a trail of debris. Their respective journeys through life will be the same.'

Contemplating this, you can draw strength from the fact that the Hause stands at 2,500 feet; fewer than a thousand now to go but it is a long trudge over stone, relieved by scarcely any greenery apart from tenacious lichen.

There are also some psychological traps. Hundreds of wayfarers assume that the prominent peak on the skyline is the summit but it isn't. It is only Ill Crag, which pokes its head well over 3,000 feet but lies two sub-summits and two cols away from the real thing. Head up, shoulders back. We have a way to go.

Calf Cove

Access to the summit ridge lies up Calf Cove, past a large cairn to the right which marks an old parish boundary, an attention to detail which pleased Wainwright as a local government officer himself. Importantly, if you are running short of water, the last opportunity to recharge your bottle comes shortly after this, where Calfcove Gill runs eastwards towards the infant river Esk. After a final stretch of manky grass, the route tops the breast of the ridge and the genuine summit can be seen for the first time. Oh dear. It seems a heck of a long way away.

Even Wainwright ran slightly short of words to describe the passing scene on this stretch; although the distant views are magnificent, the immediate surroundings consist of stones, stones and more stones. If you are familiar with T S Eliot's 'The Waste Land', you will get the idea:

What are the roots that clutch,
what branches grow
Out of this stony rubbish? Son of man,
You cannot say, or guess, for you know only
A heap of broken images, where the sun beats,
And the dead tree gives no shelter,
the cricket no relief,
And the dry stone no sound of water.

The summit is at least visible at last, with its huge round shelter-cum-cairn almost always topped by the cheerful colours of mountain walkers, but we must still go down to Ill Crag col, up to Broad Crag, down to Broad Crag col and finally up the last hundred yards to the top of the world, or at least England. Wainwright reassures us only that we should not get lost and stray over the cliffs which flank the ridge because 'the path is unmistakable, bearing the footprints and decaying litter of legions of pilgrims and an over-abundance of cairns.' There is no accounting for tastes, of course, and one of his lifelong pleasures was bivouacking overnight in a hollow just below the summit. But it was less the surroundings which attracted him than the unforgettable experience of greeting the day from the summit of the Pike in a clear dawn.

The Summit

So hooray! We are here at last, almost certainly surrounded as Wainwright predicts by 'climbers in varying degrees of exhaustion and exultation'. Weather permitting, a wonderful new view has opened up ahead of narrow Wastwater; England's deepest lake seen from England's highest mountain. Wainwright for once resists his ghoulish habit of remarking that such places are ideal for concealing dead bodies, although Wastwater was used for just this purpose in a notorious case at the end of the last century. Unfortunately for the killer, the weighted corpse came to rest on a ledge only part way down. The Isle of Man may also be shining in the far distance. On a really good day, you can see Blackpool Tower. But set aside such frivolous thoughts, for a brief but solemn ceremony of thanksgiving. You have conquered everything set before you and now it is just a matter of heading wearily down. The place you have reached may not be beautiful, but it is the ultimate in Lake District roving. As Wainwright says: 'It is the summit of England and it is fitting that it should be sturdy and rugged and strong.'

⑤ Helvellyn

Ascent from Glenridding via Striding Edge
2,750 feet of ascent
5 miles

HELVELLYN IS A great, big and basically benevolent lump which lies like an enormous whale on the Eastern side of the Lake District. It may be sentimental to attribute personal characteristics to a mountain, but many walkers do and Alfred Wainwright was one of them. The summit can be a terrifying place in foul weather, as he acknowledged, which is only to be expected of the third-highest place in England, after the two Scafells. But Helvellyn seems to have a basic good nature which has survived the indignity of ascents by almost every means known to man, including pony-carts, tractors and an Avro Avian 585 two-seater biplane.

This touched down on the gravelly, domed plateau 40 yards south of the summit on 22 December 1926, a cold wintry day when there was a dusting of snow on the high fells. A celebrated test pilot called Bert Hinkler was on board, with a Lancashire gardener and bee-keeper, John F Leeming actually at the controls. Leeming was a passionate crusader for air travel, who built a glider in his garage, founded a company called Northern Airlines and built the first municipal airport in Britain, in Manchester in 1928. The perilous landing, which left the plane only 30 yards for take-off above Red Tarn's screes, was his idea as a publicity stunt for flying. It succeeded brilliantly thanks to the presence on the summit of the professor of Greek at Birmingham University.

He was out for a pre-Christmas climb and agreed happily to witness the bizarre arrival of the two flyers which otherwise might not have been believed. Hinkler, who was also the second person after Charles Lindbergh to fly the Atlantic solo, produced an old bill from his flying jacket and wrote out a certificate which the Professor signed. Then the airmen swung their propellor and the plane trundled off, lurching down alarmingly above the tarn before pulling away and up round the side of Catstycam to release the news to the papers.

Striding Edge

We will take a much longer route but one with plenty of drama because it snakes along the longest and most famous ridge for walkers in Lakeland, Striding Edge. This is the most dramatic feature on the shattered eastern approaches to Helvellyn, which contrast so completely with the rounded, grassy humps on the west above Grasmere, Thirlmere and the pass of Dunmail Raise. Helvellyn is like a whale but also resembles a wave, rising smoothly from the west and then breaking in a chaos of precipes, combes and ridges as its eastern slopes drop down to Ullswater.

The best place to start is the bustling village of Glenridding which has plenty of parking, places to stay and shops that sell everything from picnic provisions to the latest, startlingly expensive boots. The path leads out of the village in front of the main row of shops and soon becomes an enticing track beneath trees. Watch for a wooden signpost up left marked 'Lanty's Tarn', which takes a narrow path over a stream and then on up rocky steps through woodland and out onto the fellside where it slopes right and then hairpins left.

At the top of this stretch, you can climb straight on a little further to the knobbly outcrop of Keldas, a fine viewpoint over the southern tip of Ullswater. But the main path drops slightly to the right to Lanty's Tarn, half-hidden amid stands of conifers and once the haunt of a moonshine liquor smuggler called Lanty Slee. The track runs clearly downhill past the tarn's dam and out of the trees to the brackeny fellside above Grisedale where the old packhorse route between Ullswater and Grasmere marches along the far side of the beck. Watch out, shortly before a dry-stone wall, for a path sidling off to the right through the bracken towards a small copse of trees and then slanting up the hillside.

This is the highway to Helvellyn, a very long but pleasant march at an angle across the flank of Birkhouse Moor, the main east ridge of Helvellyn and a considerable fell in its own right, reaching 2,350 feet at its dull, grassy summit.

Grisedale

The view to the left is Lakeland at its best, the narrow valley of Grisedale whose pastures slowly dwindle into rough intakes and then to rocky, bracken-clad slopes leading up to the distant pass. On the far side of this idyllic enclave, where blue woodsmoke coils from the chimneys of the last farm below Helvellyn, Elm How, is the graceful ridge of St Sunday Crag. In places it falls sheer towards the gentle valley, and you may be able to make out the zigzag route to its summit which starts just beyond Elm How, a frontal assault with none of the subtlety of our gradual ascent. Grisedale's unspoiled beauty owes much to the Matson Ground estate run by the Scott family, who bought large tracts of wild country and preserved it for the rest of us. Tenant farmers benefit, and some of the remoter properties including Elm How are holiday lets, advance bases for a spell of walking in the high fells.

The Hole in the Wall

Our objective is the Hole in the Wall, marked as such on the Ordnance Survey's maps and exactly what it says. A big dry-stone wall crosses the ridge from south to north and at the top, on the flattish spine of Birkhouse Moor, it has a large hole in it. Walkers can march through three abreast onto a stonier plateau strewn with increasingly large boulders. The exciting bit is about to begin. This is a good place for a swig of water or a spot of elevenses, to gather strength and nerve for the Edge which starts at the top of the short slope from the Hole and runs for the

From **The Western Fells** by A. Wainwright

best part of a mile to Helvellyn's summit. The ridge gradually narrows but with a good path on the right-hand side, until at an obvious rock tower called High Spying How – the highest point on the edge – it springs its best shot. An arête of slabby rock is the way ahead, where sliding forward on your bottom is the best way of progress for anyone hesitant, although the ridge top is comfortably wide enough to walk along if you do not mind heights.

Red Tarn

The drop on the Red Tarn side is not fearsome

anyway. The precipices falling away into Nethermost Cove are the ones which keep the mountain rescue busy. The sense of airiness from a basically safe viewpoint is, however, terrific and, if you are romantic, there is a sheaf of fine poems to choose from for an impromptu recital. Sir Walter Scott, for example, wrote a fine, sentimental piece about the stricken wayfarer Charles Gough, an artist from Manchester who lost his footing in 1805 and plunged to his death from the Edge. His dog stayed faithfully by his corpse for three months which is what appealed to Scott. He starts magnificently: 'I climbed the dark brow of the mighty Helvellyn, Lakes and mountains beneath me gleamed misty and wide...' Just what we are doing and seeing. Wordsworth was often here too, climbing the mountain one day in 1802 with his sister Dorothy, who wrote in her diary simply: 'Helvellyn! Glorious, glorious, glorious!' He also wrote a poem about Gough and his dog, entitled 'Fidelity', which includes this memorable couplet about Red Tarn: 'There sometimes doth a leaping fish, Send through the tarn a lonely cheer.' There actually is a rare species of fish in the tarn called the Schelley, but you are most unlikely to hear any of them give a lonely cheer. They are protected by law, like the Lake District's other curious fish the Vadence, which lives only in Lake Bassenthwaite, further north beyond Keswick. Scientists debate whether it and the Schelley were brought to these lonely outposts by predatory birds picking up roe in the species' other few habitats and dropping it off here.

A memorial to Gough and his dog stands at the point on the edge of Helvellyn summit where gasping and sweating conquerors of Striding Edge scrabble up a tedious slope of scree to reach the top. But you are not there yet. The narrow side path, which accompanies the arête, now crosses over to the left-hand side of the ridge, above Nethermost Cove, and leads through the shattered rocks of a second tower to the one awkward moment, a short drop down. This is entirely safe and not exposed to the precipices, and anyway you will be taking care after passing the metal cross which marks another fatal fall, that of a fox hunter from Patterdale called

Robert Dixon who was following foxhounds in 1858. This is often missed by walkers, but makes a useful handhold while you gaze on the desolate, silent hollows of Nethermost Cove.

Then it's up the scree, a sting in the tail if you are tired and there's the summit, a couple of hundred yards away to the right up a gentle slope and marked by a surprisingly modest heap of stones amid a small desert of shale. Halfway there, the much bigger and more obvious structure is an excellently designed shelter whose cross shape provides a bit of peace and calm whichever the way the wind is blowing. Unfortunately you can usually tell which segment is the one to crouch in or curl up on the stone bench, because it is already packed with other walkers. Helvellyn is much the most popular fell in Lakeland, which is why it also has the highest accident rate and some of the most serious problems of footpath erosion. On a clear day in summer there can be 500 or more walkers on the edge in clear weather, with queues at High Spying How and the dodgy bit on the final tower.

When Coleridge came this way in the early 1800s, he called it 'a prodigious wilderness' and contemporary prints showed golden eagles circling over Red Tarn. An eagle is extremely unlikely today, although England's last, lonely example of the species sometimes patrols here from his bachelor roost at the head of Mardale and Haweswater reservoir. The attraction now is the large colony of ravens which perform spectacular acrobatics, especially in gusty weather when they soar between Striding and Swirral Edges and then dive vertically towards the tarn, pulling out at the last moment and winging it for the precipices cackling at one another.

Brownrigg Well

Provided that it isn't too windy and chilly, the dome of Helvellyn is interesting to explore, seeking out the Hinkler and Gough memorials. If you are thirsty, Wainwright also tracks down the freshwater spring of Brownrigg Well, 500 yards west-southwest of the summit, straight towards the bump on the distant horizon which is Pillar, the giant of the Western fells. Wainwright was not to visit that for his surveying for another ten years; now his steps headed north up the curve of the summit plateau to the Ordnance Survey trig point on the spur of the summit, which leads towards Swirral Edge. This is the most exciting way back down to Glenridding, starting with a steep, rocky staircase and an invigorating scramble. Swirral is much shorter than Striding Edge but has a similar sense of exposure and excitement. The circuit known as 'Helvellyn by the edges' is a classic.

Keppel Cove and Greenside

The other great pleasure of the mountain top is the view; Helvellyn is so high that this is completely circular and the nearby, shapely pyramid of Catstycam is low enough not to hide what lies beyond. But you need to head down Swirral Edge and round the side of Catstycam to find a final surprise: the ravaging of the fell's lower slopes in Keppel Cove and Greenside by mining for silver and lead. Until you reach the despoiled valley, it seems inconceivable that thousands of people once toiled here, that the world's first electric locomotive was installed in this wilderness, and that the bursting of the mine's dam in 1927 sent a six-foot-high wall of water through Glenridding, sweeping furniture all the way across Ullswater to the foot of Place Fell. Once amid the vast desolation, with ironwork, wooden shuttering and other debris strewn around from work which ended only in 1962, the history is all too credible.

⑥ Catbells

Ascent from Hawse End
1,250 feet of ascent
1½ miles

CATBELLS IS A fairy-tale mountain which demands a special approach, so let's leave our things in Keswick and set out with walking gear and a picnic for the ferry to Hawes End. The Keswick Launch Company operates graceful wooden craft from the town's boat landings and it is only two stops to the foot of the fell, past the wooded hummocks of Lord's and St Herbert's islands.

Seen from Derwentwater on a still day, the mountain's sinuous spine doubles in size, through its reflection in the water. The sloping ridge with its distinctive crest is as inviting as you could wish, and it is no surprise that it has been the setting for many stories. The most famous involves that bustling hedgehog Mrs Tiggy-winkle, a character who is perpetually rolling up her sleeves or the hedgehog's equivalent, to get on with the laundry and other daily chores. Her creator, Beatrix Potter, had a friend in the Newlands valley which lies on the other side of Catbells, a little girl called Lucie to whom she originally told the story. One of the book's illustrations shows the fair-haired child toddling along a bracken-fringed path which you can still trace on the fell's western flank. For sceptical readers who think that Lucie's afternoon tea with Mrs Tiggy-winkle was a dream, Potter writes in conclusion: 'Besides, I have seen that door into the back of the hill called Cat Bells – and besides I am very well acquainted with dear Mrs Tiggy-winkle.' If you are bringing children, there are plenty of burrows which satisfactorily fit the bill.

Derwentwater

With the fell still distant, it is worth scanning the islets of Derwentwater, an unusually shallow lake which is always the first in the Lake District to freeze. Lord's Island was once the summer home of the Earls of Derwentwater, an aristocratic family whose power came to an abrupt end when James Radclyffe, the third Earl, sided with the Jacobites, hoping to restore the Stuart dynasty to the English throne. He lost a battle, at Preston in 1715, and three months later his head at Tower Hill. A romantic character, he was the illegitimate grandson of Charles II via the King's affair with a London singer, Moll Davis, who visited the 'pleasure house' kept on the island by her daughter Mary, the earl's mother. Samuel Pepys's wife Elizabeth called her 'the most impertinent slut in the world' and she was notorious for showing off trinkets given her by the King. Mistresses tended to have a sell-by date, however, and Moll was spectacularly undone by Nell Gwynne, who took over her role after slipping a powerful laxative into Moll's pudding at a supper. As Moll's biographer puts it: 'That night in the Royal bed did not go as planned.'

You have probably already unwittingly seen what remains of the Lord's Island pleasure house. It was dismantled in 1813 and the stones used to build the Moot Hall in Keswick's Market Square, which is now the local tourist information centre. St Herbert's island, the largest of the four in the lake, has an entirely different reputation from its raffish neighbour. It was the retreat of an Anglo-Saxon saint, a great friend of St Cuthbert of Lindisfarne, who retired here in the middle of the 7th century AD, according to the Venerable Bede's *Ecclesiastical History of the English People* 'to avoid the intercourse of man, and that nothing might withdraw his attention from unceasing mortification and prayer'. Some ruins remain alongside a folly hermitage built by Sir Wilfrid Lawson in the time of Wordsworth, whose 'The Hermit of Derwentwater' urges: 'Stranger! not unmoved, Wilt thou behold this shapeless heap of stones, The desolate ruins of St. Herbert's Cell.' If you want to do this, there are trips to the island, which like Catbells has been 'Beatrixed' onto the tourism map. It was the writer's model for Owl Island, which the squirrels visit in *The Tale of Squirrel Nutkin*. A Mass is held there every year, usually on Easter Saturday, except in rough weather when the congregation meets on the shore beneath Catbells.

This is where the launch now pulls in, dropping us for the start of a gentle and delightful climb along the fell's bony ridge to the rocky summit crest. Wainwright invited children and grandparents to follow him on this expedition, although his own unhappy family arrangements denied him such pleasures which, on a sunny summer's day, you are likely to witness all along the way. Veterans plod steadily upwards while children circle around the grassy slopes like so many collies, watched, chided or urged on to look for Mrs Tiggy-winkle's burrow by accompanying grown-ups. The climb 'is rewarding out of all proportion to the small effort needed', writes Wainwright in Book Six, *The North Western Fells*. 'Even the name has a magic challenge.'

But a warning: as he goes on to say, Catbells is not quite as innocuous as it looks and there are hazards, especially for Tiggy-winkle hunters who stray far away from the path. The sleek green slopes hide abandoned mineworkings above Little Town in Newlands – Lucie's farmhouse home – and on the fellside running down to Derwentwater. In 1962, two years before Wainwright published Book Six, there

was a fatal fall down an old shaft and there have been other accidents since. The perky crest also drops away in crags and minor precipices to Newlands. This is a heavily visited tourist mountain which is often conquered by novices in sandals or heels, who carry everything they need in a supermarket plastic bag; but you still need to take care.

Mart Bields

The path leaves the launch's landing stage at Hawse End through trees including a fine Scots Pine which Wainwright singles out on his map. It then passes through a clearing with a view of our eventual destination, Catbell's summit, to the road which circles Derwentwater and can sometimes be busy. Turn right here, and then promptly left and upwards on a path through more trees with a stone wall on your right. At the top a cattle grid marks the point where an old green road used by stock-herders slants off left onto the open fellside. This was once the hunting ground

of wild cats and martens based in the lakeside woods, which probably gave their name to the mountain, originally as Cat Bields, the shelter of the wild cat. The crags below the summit above Little Town are known as Mart Bields, which suggests the presence of martens in the past, although etymologists as usual disagree with one another about such theories.

The official route ignores the green road and stomps straight ahead, but Wainwright discovered one of his favourite zigzags a little way up the green road. Striking off to the right up the hillside, it is unusual in being one man's deliberate creation rather than a path created over centuries by shepherds or mineworkers. Sir John Woodford was an army major-general who had a summer home at Derwent Bay near the launch landing. A veteran of Waterloo, he had experience of digging trenches and making defences, and he engineered this little path to use on excursions from his home. 'His name deserves to remembered,' says Wainwright, 'by those who use this enchanting stairway.'

Catbells   1481'

Cat Bells
(two words)
on Ordnance maps

from Derwentwater

• Portinscale
• Keswick

• Stair

▲ CATBELLS
• Little Town
▲ MAIDEN MOOR
• Grange
MILES
0   1   2   3   4

from the Portinscale path

From The North Western Fells by A. Wainwright

Woodford's steps lead easily to the main route up the backbone of Catbells, which rises gently to the first of the mountain's two crests, passing a memorial to Thomas Leonard bolted to a rock. Leonard was a Methodist minister in the Lancashire mill town of Colne, who pioneered country holidays for families in the industrial centres of 19th-century Britain. An ardent advocate of fresh-air virtues, he is known as the 'father of hiking', responsible for getting the Ramblers' Association under way. Catbells is an appropriate place to honour such a man, whose many beneficiaries included families from Alfred Wainwright's home town of Blackburn.

Brandlehow

The walking is blissful now; a clear path along a long saddle, like a miniature version of the Malvern Hills with the mountain falling away steeply but grassily on both sides. After the first summit, the path drops briefy to a col where on the left we can see the upper workings of the old Brandlehow copper and lead mine. The scars of this run down to Derwentwater and are best avoided, because the levels lead to unstable tunnels and deep shafts, but their history is fascinating. The first miners, during the reign of Elizabeth I, were 74 Germans under the leadership of a Daniel Hechstetter, who built a landing stage on Derwentwater in 1567 and called it Midingstett after a village in their own country. Another inlet was soon known as Copperheap Bay as locals joined in the modest equivalent of a gold rush, which had some of the social effects of today's mobile labour market within the European Union. According to legend, the fair-haired and blue-eyed Germans played havoc with the young women of Keswick and surroundings, to the extent that they were initially coralled on Derwent Island, crossing to the foot of Catbells only for their shifts in the underground workings known as Hechstetter's Nick. But they must have escaped, because many stayed, married local women and settled down, as the number of German names in local church records shows.

Mining ended at Brandlehow in 1892 with

the final failure of years of struggle against flooding in the warren, which by then was more than 500 feet deep and stretched for over two miles. But the rich language of the industry survives in words such as wad and plumbago for graphite, sop for a seam and kibble for the heavy wooden buckets which lifted ore or bailed water from the shafts. Detailed maps of Catbells are also dotted with the traces and names of the mines, and the whole story is very well told in the Pencil Museum in Keswick.

Hugh Walpole

Also on the Derwentwater side, directly below the col, is a pleasant Victorian house in a stand of trees near the lake called Brackenburn, former home of the tireless romantic novelist Hugh Walpole, who called it 'this enchanted place, this paradise on Catbells'. His stories about the curly-haired heartbreaker Rogue Herries and his beautiful, feisty daughter Judith Paris were followed breathlessly by thousands of readers in the early and mid-20th century. Swords rang, bosoms heaved and horses galloped over the fells. Walpole's fellow writer J B Priestley, seldom a generous critic, considered that there was 'not one tired, listless page... This is fiction running on all six cylinders and of staggering horse power.' The psychologist Carl Jung was also a fan, but not everyone agreed and Walpole gradually went out of fashion, especially after Somerset Maugham guyed him mercilessly as the scheming literary opportunist Alroy Kear in *Cakes and Ale*. He was consoled by a knighthood and a long retirement gazing out at the beguiling view which you are enjoying now. A memorial plaque was placed after his death in 1941 on the fellside just above Brackenburn, which is now a B&B whose grounds laid out by Walpole are open occasionally under the National Gardens Scheme.

There is little more to do, but it is Alpine walking in miniature; a satisfyingly clear ridge and a perky summit cone reached by a rocky stairway after a grassy slope where tempting paths lead down to Derwentwater in the west and Newlands valley in the east. The path is unmistakable thanks to the tread of hundreds of thousands of boots, wellies, trainers and probably stiletto heels – this is a popular place. Not just with humans either. The local sheep have an inherited familiarity with hikers' picnics and where to find them. Don't leave your rucksack open or lying around.

The particular pleasure of the view is the presence of a foreground on either side, far below, as well as the distant panorama of other mountains. Catbells may be small, but as you have discovered it is steep, and its two main flanks drop away abruptly with no curving shoulders to obscure the view. It is also plain from here that what seemed to be a distinct summit from the clearing near Hawse End jetty is really just a characterful rise on the ridge of a much bigger mountain, Dale Head. Once rested, walkers out for the day will usually tramp onwards to this 2,473-foot summit via two further subsidiary fells, Maiden Moor and High Spy, and then curve westwards to Hindscarth and the rest of a splendid eight-mile horseshoe known as the Newlands Round. Alternatively, you can enjoy Mrs Tiggy-winkle's playground for hours, especially if you have children who enjoy 'bottoming' down grassy slopes using themselves as sledges – while keeping well clear of fenced mineworkings. Back in the valley, a celebration of the walk may be suitably rounded off with a pint of Catbells Pale Ale from the Lake District brewery at Hesket Newmarket, which was saved from closure several years ago when drinkers and villagers united to set up a rural co-operative.

⑦ Bowfell

Ascent from Langdale via Crinkle Crags
2,900 feet of ascent
5 miles

WHEN I FLOP in my living room at the end of a day's work, I often look up above the fire and mantelpiece at a painting by the Lake District artist William Heaton Cooper of mighty Bowfell. It was given to me by my wife long ago, when Heaton Coopers cost a fraction of their price today. But Bowfell has not changed. Just a glance at that proud crest of a summit has me searching for my diary and looking for a free weekend to spend in the Lakes. Bowfell and the Crinkles are always high on our list of walks.

It means leaving Leeds at daybreak, because you need an early start and clear weather for this expedition into some of Lakeland's highest fells. Given both, the rewards are tremendous. But if mist or a drenching threatens then it is prudent to turn back and take consolation in the beauties of Langdale, or content yourself with the modest climb up Pike o' Blisco. The challenging, rocky ridge of the Crinkles, with its added uncertainties caused by the local rock's effects on magnetic compass accuracy, is no place to be when the weather turns sour. Nor are the beetling cliffs of Bowfell.

Our objective is a grand and massive pyramid which stands at the head of three of Lakeland's finest valleys and close to a fourth, in every way a worthy neighbour of the loftiest land in England on the nearby Scafells. It is the only one of Wainwright's six favourite mountains which he revealed in advance of the league table he published in 1966 in the last of the *Pictorial Guides*. Six years earlier, at the end of his introduction to 20 pages on the peak in Book Four, he writes: 'Rank Bowfell among the best half-dozen', adding in a footnote that the other five would have to wait for their accolade until his work was done.

The summits of Bowfell and the five Crinkles boast a bravura display of wild rock scenery, including a vast tilting slab and a tiny cave which is officially ranked as the highest space ever to be occupied regularly in England. Our way to it clambers past a series of dramatic ravines and then along the Crinkles' serrated and complex rock towers and gullies which Wainwright, unusually liberal with his superlatives in this corner of the Lakes, captions with the line: 'Introducing Lakeland's best ridge mile.' Study of his mapping of both fells reveals a range of different routes, including an easy one for anyone who can be dropped off from a car or bus on the Wrynose Pass, or leave their car in one of the very limited off-road parking spaces there. Our journey is more arduous but more exciting. It starts at the farmhouse of Stool End, an idyllic place at the head of Langdale even if its name (probably a version of 'style') prompts schoolboy smirks.

Brown Howe

The intakes here earned notoriety following 2005's London bombings, when it was revealed that MI6 agents watched terrorist suspects in fitness training camps on the fellside, an abuse of this heavenly area if ever there was one. The path heads up the side valley of Oxendale from the farm buildings before cutting left towards Brown Howe, a grassy shoulder above the ravines cut by Browney Gill. Amid the customary rowan trees and banks of bracken above the tumbling stream, look out for traces of red soil. The ground is rich in minerals along the Crinkles and around Bowfell, notably at Ore Gap where a large vein of haematite comes close to the surface. This may partly account for the problems with compasses hereabouts, uniquely in the Lake District.

The path to Brown Howe traverses a steep succession of contour lines, from 500 to 1,600 feet, and is the day's most concentrated climb, a stretch to interrupt with rests to gaze backwards down the dale. One of the delights of the whole walk is the succession of contrasts between the increasingly wild terrain of the upper fells, and the peaceful green fields of the farms behind and below. The growing sense of wilderness as you climb higher is enhanced by the boulders strewn about the narrow bed of both Oxendale beck and Browney gill. In spate the streams become furious torrents, sweeping away such obstacles as the footbridge by a sheepfold which takes our path across Oxendale beck. It was only reinstalled in 2005.

At a particular concentration of red soil beneath the cliffs of Great Knott on the right, the valley splits into two dramatic ravines and the path skirts to the left and a final haul up to Red Tarn, the lonely stretch of water on the col between Pike o' Blisco on the left and the Crinkles to the right. More red soil and a patch of reddish scree mark the start of the hike to the Crinkles crest, the five towers which make such a striking coxcomb from upper Langdale. They are every bit as rocky and jumbled as they look from a distance, particularly if you venture carefully off the main path, which is well marked for most of the way by the boot scuffs and nail scratches of your many predecessors. At the start of this section, for instance, a diversion to the right takes you to the edge of the crags of Grey Knott and then turns left up a short scree gully, parallel to the main ridge path, to Gladstone's Finger, a striking pinnacle which appears to beckon rock climbers – but definitely not walkers – to clamber up to its narrow tip.

The Bad Step

The diversion bears slightly left after the finger to rejoin the main path, with enticing glimpses of the second and third Crinkle. The first of the five towers is traversed without difficulty and then a gentle dip leads to the second and highest, a cracked dome of rock which hides the one insurmountable obstacle for many walkers on the ridge. The apparently obvious way up, a gash of scree on the side of the tower, ends in a boulder choke called the Bad Step; ten feet of vertical ascent and technically a rock climb. The usual policy is to divert to the left, up an easy rake which leads to the 2,816-foot second Crinkle over a substance which has become rare in the stony panorama, green grass. Wainwright's fellow guide to the Lake District, the *Guardian* Country Diary writer Harry Griffin, regularly mocked the Bad Step, claiming that thousands had scampered over it without a second

thought 'until Wainwright made such a meal of it'. The best policy is to go and look carefully for yourself, but bear in mind that Griffin was a skilful and experienced rock climber.

The second Crinkle is the summit of the fell, and the three remaining are clearly the supporting cast; but a sense of things still to do is imposed by the sight of Bowfell rising majestically beyond. The path continues along the short summit ridge known as Long Top which conceals the highest source of fresh water in the Lake District, a

spring which trickles into action only after recent rain. Like a grey stone roller-coaster, the route then dips across the head of Mickledoor, a wide scree gully down to Oxendale and Langdale, and scrambles up boulders to the top of the third Crinkle, one of the best viewpoints over the sweet valleys below. The last two Crinkles drop in succession, each after a rocky gap, with the path clambering along to the left and short diversions needed to claim the actual tops. Both have similar wonderful views.

Three Tarns

So the Crinkles are conquered. The ridge now drops past two small mountain tarns down to the well-trodden crossroads before Bowfell, where Three Tarns (or more accurately two and a half) lie in the dip. Your boots are back on peaty soil and grass after the mile of rock; but not for long. If the Crinkles were an exhilarating scramble, even better things lie ahead along the Climbers' Traverse, one of those Wainwright specialities which take the walker off the beaten track and into the exciting domain of the 'crag rats', climbers who inch and finger-jam their way up frighteningly sheer cliffs. Our role is only as spectators; not exactly armchair climbers, but ones who are going to stick safely to a clear but exciting rock path.

The traverse leaves the often-busy route from Langdale via The Band to Bowfell a short distance below Three Tarns on the Langdale side. In the event of bad weather or if the Crinkles have been enough for one day, this is the place to turn back to the valley, completing a lovely circuit. Wainwright's route down Buscoe Sike and along the edge of Hell Gill ravine (stay well above the stream, whose bed is impassable) turns right off the main path, just beyond the left turn to the Climbers' Traverse. It is a consistent delight, passing the fine, hidden waterfall of Whorneyside Force before it reaches Stool End.

Bowfell   2960'

'Bow Fell' (two words)
on Ordnance Survey maps

from Lingmoor Fell

From The Southern Fells by A. Wainwright

But onwards to Bowfell; not much height is lost below Three Tarns before you swing left off the path down to Langdale, and onto a contour track across rocks and scree.

This clings to the steep slope below foreboding cliffs above Mickleden until a great tower of rock called Cambridge Crag reaches down to the level of the path, clearly identifiable not merely by its size but because a spring of icy cold water gushes from its base. 'Nothing better ever came out of a barrel or bottle,' says Wainwright, who declared himself overawed by the mountain scenery all around. While the valley below looks as gentle and reassuring as ever, the surrounding cliffs are savage and apparently impenetrable. Beyond Cambridge Crag stands the magnificent pyramid of Bowfell Buttress, armoured with sheets of unbroken rock where the climbers specialise in finding hairbreadth cracks and all but invisible holds. The main face of the buttress only fell to their efforts in 1902.

Beyond and into the North Gully is strictly their domain. The scramblers' path ('although grandmothers and infants may consider it prudent to turn back here.' warns Wainwright) returns to the base of Cambridge Crag and strikes steeply up the scree between Cambridge and Flat Crags. Be careful. Even Wainwright admitted upsetting a large boulder from its socket on the top of Cambridge Crag so that it wedged his other foot. He managed to shift it back unaided, but shuddered at the ignominy that would have been involved, after his many years of advocating solitary fellwalking, in shouting for help to the tourist path to Bowfell summit which passes just above.

The Great Slab

The upper side of Flat Crag has one of the finest sights in Lakeland's rock landscape, a vast area of tilted stone which Wainwright accurately calls the Great Slab. He drew it several times, using one version on the cover of *Fellwanderer* and another in the *Pictorial Guides* (the little figure at the top of the slab, gazing down, is slightly more decrepit in the latter and has a stick). The slab can be walked across, but take care and keep well above its lower edge. At the top, a sort of parapet leads to a short stretch of boulders and the main

path to Bowfell summit from Three Tarns. A short diversion down this to the left reveals a view of the col and a series of up to a dozen parallel scree gullies down to it, which form an unexpectedly geometrical feature in the chaotic landscape, and are known as the Links of Bowfell.

The summit is a steep but brief final haul over stony ground littered with boulders. It falls just short of 3,000 feet at 2,960 feet, but has a lonely grandeur (crowds of hikers permitting) and stupendous views. A line of cairns, invaluable in mist, leads on to Ore Gap and the neighbouring fell of Esk Pike but Bowfell's true – and obvious – top is just up to the left. As Wainwright says, showing his consistent admiration of stone piles on the summits of Lakeland, the peak is 'a giant cairn in itself, a great heap of stones and boulders and naked rock'. Make sure you have *The Southern Fells* with you, because its 360-degree panorama over four pages of the view from here is invaluable for spotting dozens of peaks – the Mickledore gap between Scafell and Scafell Pike is particularly dramatic – or resolving arguments.

The 'highest house'

The final delight, which must be carried out cautiously, is to inspect the broken ground above the precipices of Bowfell Buttress, viewing from above the awesome slopes which on the Climbers' Traverse you gazed at from below. Hidden in this jumble on a rather exposed ledge above the climbers' favourite of North Gully is the 'highest house', a smuggler's cave so small that you can only squeeze in bottom first. It is probably best left to the experts; but to miss the general view of the crags as many sadly do, says Wainwright, is to miss half the glories of Bowfell.

⑧ Pillar

Ascent from Black Sail via the
High Level Traverse
2,100 feet of ascent
3 miles

PILLAR IS A mountain name which brings goosebumps to two different sorts of people. First, the rock-climbing 'crag rats' whose exploits on the soaring buttress above Ennerdale have made the great crag of Pillar Rock legendary; indeed, this is where their sport began. Then there are the armchair explorers — perhaps all of us at one time or other — who love to read of daring deeds in such lonely and dangerous places, but in comfort and from a considerable distance.

Thanks in large part to Wainwright, the beetling precipices of the most formidable crag in the Lake District have now become familiar to a third category — the fellwalker, who loves to be in such high, wild spots but does not want to break a leg in the process. This climb up Pillar mountain's 2,927 feet takes us into the very heart of the climbers' domain, so close that we will touch the sheer stone edges of Shamrock and Pisgah, two of the Rock's outlying fortresses, and feel for ourselves the wispy grooves which the crag rats use to hoist themselves up like flies on a vast wall. The High Level Traverse, a thread of a climbers' path, was popularised for walkers by Wainwright. It clambers over boulders and scree to the foot of the cliffs, then tracks upwards to the summit on a stony ladder, scuffed with the marks of boots and nails, which is the one chink in the mountain's defences above the wastes of the upper reaches of Ennerdale.

To tackle this dramatic route, it is fitting to start from another shrine among Lake District mountaineers, the remote youth hostel of Black Sail which itself can only be reached by a long walk — nearly nine miles from Ennerdale Bridge or five if you park at Bowness Knot on the north bank of Ennerdale Water where the public road comes to an end. There are quicker approaches to Pillar, from Wasdale Head, Honister Pass (both with parking) or directly from Ennerdale Water up the side of Black Crag to Wind Gap above Mirk Cove — but what a trio of deservedly intimidating names! Wainwright dutifully describes these alternatives in his seventh and final volume of the *Pictorial Guide, The Western Fells*; but Black Sail has a magic of its own and a night in its simple bunkhouse bedrooms — maximum 16 people — is a memorable Lakeland experience. It can be unintentionally memorable, it should be added, if anyone in the party snores.

Wild Ennerdale

The haul to Black Sail from Ennerdale Bridge is long but gentle and rewarded by a lovely walk beside Ennerdale Water, especially if you follow Wainwright's Coast to Coast route along the very edge of the southern shore. The three extra miles compared with parking at Bowness Knot are worth it. After Robin Hood's Seat there is an easy scramble, and then the path winds through a wood of stunted trees before crossing the dancing river Liza into the dark conifer plantations which Wainwright hated. Their day is almost done; the higher reaches of the forest have recently been harvested and more enlightened planting is mixing the types of tree. The regiments are breaking up, and the arrival of more sunlight has added to the variety of animals and plants. If you are very lucky, you may see a pine marten slink through the upper branches, but this remains a rare treat.

The Forestry Commission is one of the three partners in Wild Ennerdale, a project which would have been dear to Wainwright's heart. Together with the water company United Utilities and the National Trust, it is returning Ennerdale to the status of 'wild valley'. From suffering sneers as an area ruined by exploitation, the narrow but grand highway to Pillar and Great Gable is changing into an exemplar of good green practice. Visitors are welcome but not in cars, and there will be no artificial attractions, not even tearooms. Hostel laundry is likely to be done in the infant Liza, and the wind turbine already mounted on the hostel's roof will be increased in power.

However high-minded your feelings about such simple ways, it is very pleasant to see Black Sail, beds, loos and all, when you round the last corner in the forestry track. The former shepherds' bothy tucks snugly into the side of Haystacks, with a sheep-trimmed lawn on its lap like an apron, before the land rolls off into hummocks of coarse grass. The surroundings are utterly spectacular. Gable towers above the end of the valley, Kirk Fell to its right and Green Gable left; three judges on a court bench, complete with wigs of snow in winter, waiting to deliver their verdict on the best you can do. The hut itself has a rich history right up to the present time; a plaque inside commemorates the final visit of the Olympic gold medallist Chris Brasher, who chose to come to Black Sail with a party of friends when he knew that terminal cancer could no longer be fought.

Although the remotest of English youth hostels, the bothy has a fine reputation for hospitality. In recent years the wardens, who seldom stay but commute in from Ennerdale, have acquired an international reputation for hot curries and a remarkable cellar (or at least cupboard) of wines. International is the correct adjective. Black Sail is known among walkers all over the world and is also the most famous overnighter on the Coast to Coast. After nightfall in peaceful weather, the lonely valley fills with two great rarities of modern life: velvet darkness and complete silence. Sit on the lawn, or the bench in memory of the Leeds youth worker who brought thousands of lucky children here, and absorb the peace. The stars gradually appear and, as your pupils adjust into great dark circles, so do the outlines of the fells. That's where you're off out in the morning.

Sail Beck

Sally forth cheerfully, because a fair amount of your job is already done. Black Sail is a classic advance camp. Much of the grandeur of Pillar lies in its remoteness and you have secured a base nearly a thousand feet up its flanks. The path crosses the Liza and mounts steeply but without difficulty alongside tumbling Sail

Beck. There may be moments if you suffer from poor weather when you reflect on the origin of the name Black Sail, which means 'a dark and swampy hill'. If mist threatens, it would be advisable for inexperienced walkers to change plans at this point and rest content with a lower-level walk, perhaps to Wasdale Head. If all is set fair, turn right on reaching the col, once a very well-trodden commercial route from this part of Lakeland to the Cumbrian ports, and strike out for the first of three stony rises which lead to Pillar's summit.

The High Level Traverse

Don't go too far. Pausing to gaze down Ennerdale from the grassy hummock of Looking Stead, which involves a short diversion to the right of the path, continue beside the old fence, watching out carefully for a track sloping off to the right at the foot of a line of crags which rise to the right of the main, ridge route to Pillar top. This is the High Level Traverse, and in Wainwright's words 'the start of one of the best miles in Lakeland, a route of engrossing interest'. Interest was particularly focused in past days, when the track started with a slide on your bottom over a small

but tricky rock outcrop, but a diversion now runs below this and on to a steady contour across scree. A sense of excitement is immediate and grows rapidly. Below, the fell plunges steeply away into Ennerdale with little Black Sail and its emerald apron far below. Above, the rocks get ever higher. Ahead, we know that we are very soon going to see Pillar Rock, the monarch of them all.

Robinson's Cairn

The great crag comes into view at the top of a short rise topped by Robinson's Cairn, a memorial placed in 1907 to honour John Wilson Robinson, an early cragsman who used to get up at 4am and walk 15 miles to these cliffs from his home at Whinfell Hall in Lorton and the same distance back in the evening. The plaque tells how 'one hundred of his comrades and friends' subscribed to this way of recording how Robinson 'knew and loved as none other these his native fells, whence he drew simplicity, strength and charm'. It may prompt reflections on Wainwright, so similarly knowledgeable and undoubtedly strong, but denied the other two gifts.

Robinson was a Quaker and co-founder of the Fell and Rock Climbing Club, one of those Victorian and Edwardian gents who climbed in Norfolk jackets with hemp ropes, taking risks which would have modern health and safety officers in fits. They usually holed up at the Wastwater Hotel, challenging one another to attempt the 'billiard table traverse', a circuit of the bar done without touching the floor. Wainwright's contemporary and fellow-writer Harry Griffin recalled lawyers, company directors and military officers belting out climbing songs in the 1920s while the Regius Professor of History at Oxford University kept time with a poker. The poet Geoffrey Winthrop Young was one of them, climbing with the help of a special attachment on his artificial leg. Another academic went up crags blindfold for bets. A German doctor and skinny-dipper tried to persuade the teenaged Griffin that he should never dry himself after a tarn swim, because water went back naturally into the body, restoring its energy. If true, Griffin grumbled, it took an uncomfortably long time.

Scafell Crag and the slender spire of Napes Needle on Great Gable were playgrounds near Wasdale Head for these pioneers, but Pillar Rock was their holy of holies. For it was here that British rock climbing may be said to have begun, with the first recorded ascent in 1826 by a local enthusiast called John Atkinson. He had been inspired directly by Wordsworth who wrote in 1800:

You see yon precipice; it almost looks
Like some vast building made of many crags;
And in the midst is one particular rock
That rises like a column from the vale,
Whence by our shepherds it is called the Pillar.

In proper romantic style the poem, *The Brothers*, involves a shepherd's tragic fall to his death from the rock, but that did not put Atkinson off, and he was followed by many successors.

Shamrock

From Robinson's Cairn you get a clear idea of the awesome height of the Rock, and the way that its footings are so far down the mountainside, giving a summit-to-base height of more than 500 feet. Wainwright includes three tiny figures on his drawing of the almost vertical West Face, out of sight from our dramatic-viewpoint, on the crag's far side. He also writes unequivocally about the tempting slope from Robinson's Cairn to the base of the main rock, High Man: 'This is not the way to go. To walkers whose experience is limited to easy scrambling on rough ground, Pillar Rock is positively out of bounds. Don't even try to get a foothold on it.' This is sound advice.

Walker's Gully

Instead, safely but still in wonderfully dramatic mountain scenery, the path turns left and upwards, hugging a low rocky ridge at the base of Shamrock, a subsidiary but still vast cliff in front of Pillar Rock. The name has nothing to do with plants or Irish climbers. It refers to the fact that this is a separate outcrop, split from Pillar Rock by the wildly misnamed Walker's Gully, another preserve of climbers only, which cannot be seen from here. The cliff was therefore deemed to be a 'sham rock', pretending to be part of the real thing; at close quarters, you may feel that there is very little sham about it at all.

At the top of a short scree slope, an easy but excitingly narrow ledge slopes up to the right along the top of Shamrock, with the wear and tear of previous walkers showing that this is the way to go. You are now in the heart of sheer rock country, with a close-up view of High Man at the top of the incline which may make you giddy. Wainwright employs his ultimate tribute, averring that 'even toothache can be forgotten in such sensational surroundings,' although he warns that timid visitors may find it all too much of 'a place of horror, awful and ugly'.

It is certainly not somewhere for anyone with vertigo; but, timid or not, we must scamper on from the end of the Shamrock Traverse, at the same angle but over a wider, stony slope, past the spot where the mountain rescue stretcher box stood in Wainwright's day. It was often used. Walker's Gully was actually named after a climber called Walker who fell to his death there. On one of Wainwright's own research trips here, he was hailed by a group of men far

below who were searching for a friend who had not returned from a walk on Pillar the previous day. He too was found dead at the foot of the gully. Among the boulders of Great Doup, another scree run to the left of and a little above our route, is an inconspicuous cross in memory of Rev James 'Steeple' Jackson, who conquered Pillar Rock at the age of 80 but died in a fall two years later while trying to repeat the feat. Don't go looking for it. Stick to the track.

Pillar Rock

This continues for a short distance to the foot of Pisgah, named after the mountain from which Moses was permitted to view the Promised Land but to go no further. Climbers can imitate him like the three little men in Wainwright's drawing who gaze across a great rent on the rock between Pisgah and High Man. Not us. Turn your face upwards and take the steep and rugged pathway, left from Pisgah and in a straight line to the summit of the mountain. Toil, toil, says Wainwright, albeit with grand views opening up around, but then the gradient eases and the path arrives on a grassy plateau. This is the top of Pillar, although you might consider Pancake a better name.

For the glory of Pillar lies in its Rock. As Wainwright might have remarked in one of his philosophical moments, this journey is more rewarding than its destination, as can often be the case in life. He didn't say that, because if you have got here in good time as he always did, there are fine ridge walks onwards to Kirkfell or round the Mosedale Horseshoe via Scoat Fell and the delicate pinnacle of Steeple; or you can take what he calls 'the royal road down to Wasdale Head', a descent with glorious views. If you have enough energy, you might even try the modern equivalent of the billiard table traverse in the car park or at the Wastwater Hotel.

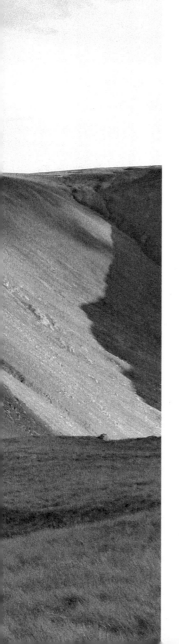

⑨ High Street

Ascent from Mardale Head via Rough Crag
2,050 feet of ascent
3 miles

THE PHRASE 'where eagles dare' was once a commonplace in Lakeland, as dozens of Eagle Crags bear witness on the remoter flanks of the fells. Today there is only one mountainside in the region where the description still applies accurately; and even here we now have to refer to 'eagle' in the singular. There is just one of the great birds left. He is the last in England, and although he has been visited by female relatives from Scotland, which as an eagle flies is not so far away, none of the recent visitors have stayed. A conservation project run with painstaking care from the old reservoir village of Burnbanks below Haweswater dam has done everything it can to encourage a breeding record, which hatched 16 young after a pair of adults returned to the valley in 1969 after almost 120 years' absence. But there have been no further mates for the ageing male since the last disappeared in 2004. Her remains were never found.

There are many other ghosts in the deserted valley from which this walk starts. Two villages were flooded when the natural lake of Haweswater was dammed and expanded by about a third between 1919 and 1935 to meet the demands of thirsty Manchester. Hundreds of thousands of gallons are now pumped south every day and the lake, one of the deepest and biggest in the national park, holds enough spare to give everyone on the planet three baths each. From the promontory called The Rigg at the head of the reservoir, you can see a whole network of underwater walls where the cottages of Mardale Green and the intakes of Riggindale Farm once stood. Most grievously of all, the dale lost its ancient pub the Dun Bull, which was a favourite place for walkers to stay or slake their thirst and have supper after a long day on these little-frequented Far Eastern fells. Manchester Corporation built the Haweswater Hotel as an alternative, complete with a welcoming Walkers' Bar, in a castellated 'Reservoir Medieval' style. But although originally intended to stand by The Rigg close to the old village site, which would have been ideal, it ended up peculiarly off the walkers' tracks, halfway down the lake on the far side.

Burnbanks

To its credit, however, the council also laid a road to the head of the new lake, and provided a car park there, which is an excellent starting point right at the foot of High Street. On the way, it is worth stopping briefly at a couple of reservoir history sites. Burnbanks' navvies' village is currently being restored in a modest way, so that the scattering of surviving prefabs in which the dambuilders were housed have been joined by smarter modern versions of the same design. Smarting from the national controversy over the planned flooding of the beautiful valley, Manchester Corporation pulled out the stops to provide model conditions when work started in 1920. The 66 hutments surrounded a small hospital, mission chapel, allotments and tennis courts, all in a woodland glade. Original cast-iron fingerposts embossed with the corporation's initials still point the way to pretty paths, including one which creeps along the western shore of Haweswater while the road takes the other side. Keen walkers with plenty of time may decide to start the assault on High Street here; the lakeside path's three miles pass a fine waterfall at Measand Force, above the second of the flooded hamlets, Measand, and the relics of an ancient British fort perched on top of a cliff below Birks Crag, the final buttress of the south-east ridge of High Raise, High Street's neighbour.

Tower Pier

On the road to Mardale Head, shortly after the Haweswater Hotel, look out on the right for a delicate little fake-medieval keep rising out of the water on the edge of the reservoir and connected to the bank by a twin-arched bridge. This is Tower Pier, actually not a pier at all but the elegantly disguised 'draw off' mechanism for the reservoir which allows United Utilities

to determine the level of flow, depending on factors such as water quality and overall depth of the lake.

From the car park, the climb proper begins amid the almost Alpine beauty of the reservoir's headwaters. Islets picturesquely planted with conifers and the hook of the final stretch of water round The Rigg form a complicated and satisfying pattern. Wainwright himself, although one of the many thousands who deplored the flooding, admitted that 'it must be conceded that Manchester has done the job as unobtrusively as possible.' The track dips down to cross Mardale beck, where a short diversion upstream is worthwhile to see the torrent squeeze through a rock fissure at Dodderwick Force. Back past the footbridge, the route goes right at a T-junction and follows the lake shore, albeit separated from it by a high dry-stone wall, until a fork amid bracken takes us left and uphill, shortly before the plantation on The Rigg.

Rough Crag

The path now strikes straight up Rough Crag, a well-defined ridge which Wainwright calls 'the connoisseur's route up High Street'. The flanks of the ridge drop away increasingly steeply on both sides, grassy to the left but rocky and tree-lined on the right above Riggindale. This is where the eagle lives, roosting on trees between Heron and Eagle Crags, the latter's name suggesting that the birds were revisiting traditional haunts in the manner of swallows when they returned in 1969. The Royal Society for the Protection of Birds runs an observation hide down in Riggindale between April and August, but you may well get your own, grandstand view from here. Once when Wainwright was on Rough Crag, the great bird took off as he came down this final stretch and soared to the crags below

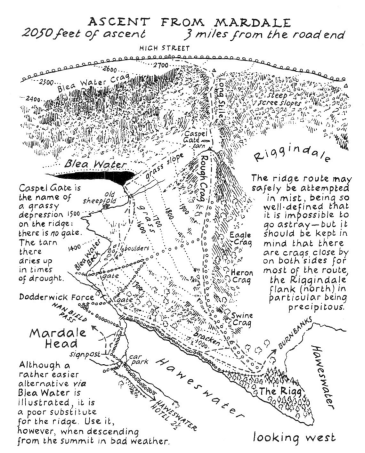

High Street 6

ASCENT FROM MARDALE
2050 feet of ascent   3 miles from the road end

HIGH STREET

2700

2600

2500

Blea Water Crag

2400

Long Stile

steep scree slopes

Caspel Gate tarn

Blea Water

grass slope

Rough Crag

Riggindale

Caspel Gate is the name of a grassy depression 1500 on the ridge: there is *no* gate. The tarn there dries up in times of drought.

old sheepfold

1500

grass

1400

1600

1700

1800

1900

boulders

Blea Water Beck

gate

Eagle Crag

Heron Crag

The ridge route may safely be attempted in mist, being so well·defined that it is impossible to go astray—but it should be kept in mind that there are crags close by on both sides for most of the route, the Riggindale flank (north) in particular being precipitous.

Dodderwick Force

NAN BIELD PASS

gate

gate

Swine Crag

Mardale Head

signpost

car park

bracken

1000

Haweswater

Although a rather easier alternative *via* Blea Water is illustrated, it is a poor substitute for the ridge. Use it, however, when descending from the summit in bad weather.

HAWESWATER HOTEL

Haweswater

The Rigg

BURN BANKS

Haweswater

looking west

The ridge of Rough Crag and the rocky stairway of Long Stile together form the connoisseur's route up High Street, the only route that discloses the finer characteristics of the fell. The ascent is a classic, leading directly along the crest of a long, straight ridge that permits of no variation from the valley to the summit. The views are excellent throughout.

From The Far Eastern Fells by A. Wainwright

Kidsty Pike, the fine little peak on a spur the far side of Riggindale, with just two beats of its wings. When I followed in his footsteps, its successor appeared, to chase off a flight of ravens which had come down from High Street's upper cliffs and were playing their usual mad games with the wind. Predictably big in wingspan, the eagle also has a hefty body for a bird and notably large legs, with yellowish talons which it puts to good use. An exaggerated reputation for taking lambs was the main reason for its extinction in England in 1850. The RSPB's work in Haweswater has shown how the Lake District eagles' diet consists much more of carrion and vermin than farm prey.

The little summit of Rough Crag is really no more than a knobble on the undulating ridge, marked by a perky cairn before the path drops to a reedy and often damp col called Caspel Gate. From the cairn, there is a view of Blea Tarn down to the left and beyond it, the beautifully positioned lesser tarn of Small Water below Nan Bield. The great bowl is framed by the precipices of Bleawater Crag, an abrupt and therefore dangerous downfall from High Street's innocuous-seeming, flat and grassy top. There have been fatal accidents among hikers there, but you can drop safely down the grassy slope from Caspel Gate to the edge of Blea Tarn.

Corpse Road

Gazing back the way we have come, the narrow valley at the head of Haweswater reveals an unexpected exit through the hills on the other side. A zigzag path climbing up from Mardale Head is the old Corpse Road along which the people of the drowned hamlet for centuries made their final journey. Until 1729 when Mardale church was built, there was no consecrated ground around Haweswater and coffins were taken eight miles for burial at Shap. One of the last official ceremonies before the reservoir waters closed in was the disinterment of remains from Mardale for reburial in new graves at Shap, alongside forebears from the village whose bodies had been carried on the Corpse Road centuries before. The church was not so reverently treated. Its stones were too useful for the construction of Haweswater dam, in which they lie interred.

The way forward now starts to climb again and there is only one option: straight ahead. The ridge narrows into a rocky staircase called Long Stile, steep but with an obvious route along the top. A final huff and puff up scree, which can be slidy, takes you to the summit plateau and an immediate and absolute change in the landscape.

Your efforts have brought you to another world; green and rolling, with the summit of High Street only a five-minute stroll to where a concrete trig point stands by a half-ruined dry-stone wall. The remains of the Roman road march away to the left and, more dramatically, descend on the right to the Straits of Riggindale. This is a narrow neck of land at the head of the eagle's valley which for me always prompts thoughts of Thermopylae or Horatius holding the bridge against the besiegers of Rome. As well as the slopes from High Street and High Raise, whose 2,634-foot summit is only 75 feet short of its neighbour's, the land drops dramatically into Riggindale and almost as steeply the other side, where you can glimpse the distant beauties of Ullswater.

The Annual Gathering

The loss of Mardale Green strikes home with particular force on the summit of High Street. The path which we have just taken with a fair amount of effort was a daily way to work for the hamlet's farmers and shepherds. Once a year it was also the highway to the local Annual Gathering, a day of festivities which, until early Victorian times, was celebrated every November in this lofty spot. Families trekked up from Mardale with barrels of beer and hampers of food, while ponies were taken up the gentler routes via Kidsty Pike or Nan Bield pass for the main event of the day, horse racing. A crude course was laid out on the plateau which is still called Racecourse Hill on the Ordnance Survey map, intriguing pathfinders who have not yet discovered the history. Everyone stayed until long after dark, and there are many stories associated with their revels. On one occasion, a locally famous foxhunter called Dixon was finishing his beer when he saw a fox skulk along the edge of Bleawater Crag and disappear over the top. Running after it in his excitement, he tumbled over and fell hundreds of feet to his death on the screes, after one last shout of 'It's gone over theer!' to help followers before he expired. It was, says Wainwright drily, 'an epic in enthusiasm'. Lakeland Dixons seem prone to this; witness Striding Edge's memorial to another who died in the same way.

The Gathering was moved to the Dun Bull in the 1840s and flourished for almost another century, for the community which was destroyed by the floods was an isolated and close one. As Wainwright frequently remarks, there is something unspoiled and special about this frontier area of the national park. Even today, you can share his experience of walking the High Street range from dawn to dusk without meeting another soul.

Loadpot Hill

In spite of the grand views and singing larks, the featureless summit of High Street comes as an anti-climax for some visitors. One remedy is to think of the tramp of legions, the sing-song merriment of the Gathering and Dixon's last, go-get-im holler. But there is also the very satisfactory thought that you have reached an aerial highway whose full exploration, almost from the upper reaches of Windermere to the far end of Ullswater, can take a whole day with only relatively modest ups and downs. The hard climbing work is done. Diversions down the flanks to both the east and west disclose lovely views of the attendant lakes, especially Ullswater, and you are very likely to be deceived into thinking, in some of the most lonely spots, that you have just found a row of small wind turbines on the skyline. Then they move. The supposed blades of a turbine are the long ears and slender nose of wild deer, which roam the northern part of the High Street massif from a well-tended sanctuary. In the rutting season, the bellowing of the stags is an additional, unexpected feature of a day on these fells. Man's organisation of the reserve and hunting has also left curious traces, including the wealth of boundary stones and the wreckage of Lowther House shooting lodge more than 2,000 feet up on the summit of Loadpot Hill. Such memories will accompany you home and give the land of the eagles a permanent place in your mind.

SARAH HUTCHINSON
The beloved S... ...
Mourners who have ...
with an earnest wish that ... ...
may be laid by her side ... ...
that, through Christ ... ...
...made Partakers of the same ... ...
SHE WAS BORN AT ...
AND DIED AT RYDAL 23... JUNE ...
In Fulfilment of that Wish ...
are now gathered near her the Remains ...
WILLIAM WORDSWORTH
Born at Cockermouth 7th April 177...
Died at Rydal 23rd April 1850.
And of
DOROTHY WORDSWORTH
Born at Cockermouth 25th December ...
Died at Rydal 25th January 18...
And finally of
MARY WORDSWORTH
Wife of WILLIAM WORDSWORTH
and Sister of SARAH HUTCHINSON
Born at Penrith August 16th ...
...ed at Rydal Mount January ...

⑩ Helm Crag

Ascent from Grasmere
1,100 feet of ascent
1 ½ miles

THE A591 ROAD between Ambleside and Keswick is one of the busiest tourist routes in the Lake District national park and has been since the days of charabanc outings in the early 20th century. Nose-to-tailing on sunny days between Wordsworth shrines and the fudge and teashops of Grasmere, its traffic always reminds me of my father, a determined non-walker, who used to quote the poet W H Auden with relish:

I like mountains too, seen from afar
I like to travel through them in a car.

Certainly, there is much beautiful scenery to be enjoyed from behind a windscreen, both in the distance and coming right up to the verges of the road; but this is hardly a favourite spot for fellwanderers.

Except... Look over Grasmere and lift your eyes a little to the hills, as instructed in the Old Testament. Something rather extraordinary and beguiling greets your gaze. What is that peculiar jumble of spikes and knobbles on top of the small but very steep, almost bristling fell which rises directly from the last outlying houses of the village? Can anyone resist the chance to find out?

The mountain is Helm Crag and it reaches only a modest 1,328 feet, but its character is out of all proportion to its height. As we shall discover, it is the only fell whose actual peak, at the top of a pinnacle of smooth rock, Alfred Wainwright failed to reach. He left a tiny space in Book Four, *The Central Fells*, to record this achievement if it ever happened, which it didn't. Alongside it is an equally miniature diagram showing Helm Crag in relation to Grasmere – essentially a triangle and a dot – which is the smallest map in the whole of the *Pictorial Guides*, as he proudly points out.

Until we reach the summit plateau and its exhilarating obstacle course of which the inaccessible pinnacle is only one part, Helm Crag is an easy and very enjoyable fellwalk. The going is good, especially over a broad shoulder of grass dotted with wildflowers such as the tiny yellow tormentil and red scarlet pimpernel. On one ascent, my wife and I met a lost racing pigeon at the bottom of the fell which accompanied us all the way to the top, mostly in pursuit of our picnic. Since we had no idea where it was bound, we could not help it much, but the summit of Helm Crag is a good place for wildlife to hunt for bits of sandwich crust and fruit peel and it may still be living there.

Grasmere

The walk starts in Grasmere which has ample parking and rather too many temptations which may detain you. Never mind; Helm Crag does not take long, and if necessary you can happily start in the early afternoon and be back before dusk, even during the short days of winter. Perhaps it would be appropriate to visit Wordsworth's grave in Grasmere churchyard, while the Wordsworth Centre based in and around his famous old home at Dove Cottage is a Lake District essential. An excellent and very interestingly designed extension has recently been added to the long-established charms of the old house, one of whose rooms the Wordsworths wallpapered with newspaper — still there and still readable. Before neighbouring houses blocked the view, the family was able to look out towards Helm Crag. Wordsworth wrote lovingly in 1802 of his

Little nook of mountain-ground...
Sweet garden-orchard, eminently fair,
The loveliest spot that man hath ever found.

In front of Dove Cottage, albeit also hidden by the later Victorian houses, is Grasmere lake where you can hire old-fashioned rowing boats with scroll-armed seats. The obvious destination is Duck Poo Island, as it is known by my family among many others. The scourge of dog mess is not found on this excellent picnic spot, but the ducks do their best to make up for it. Another attraction of Grasmere, and one which perhaps gives the best feel of the hills for novices, is the studio and art gallery devoted to the work of the Heaton Cooper family, especially the patriarch William. His skill captured the distinctive colours of Lakeland, especially the foxy russet of bracken and the washed-out straw of mountain grass. in a series of books, he also coined evocative phrases such as 'eyes of the mountain', for the many tarns high up in the fells. Time spent here will prepare you for the delights of the real thing outside.

The way to Helm Crag is up the little lane to Goody Bridge and Easedale which leaves Grasmere a little way beyond the Heaton Cooper studio on the left. You may have a fair amount of company because initially this is also the way to Easedale Tarn and the spectacular waterfall of Sour Milk Gill. Mass tourism is a venerable institution here; in the 1930s the tarn probably had more visitors than today, with pony-carts permitted and a refreshment hut on the lake shore whose ruins may still be seen. But not today. Our way branches off to the right, while the tarn-bound parties march on across Easedale beck and through pretty woods into pastureland and up the far fellside.

Allan Bank

Before this junction, a gate in the hedge to the left of the lane, opposite a small housing estate, leads to much easier going than the tarmac, along the edge of a field. The big house

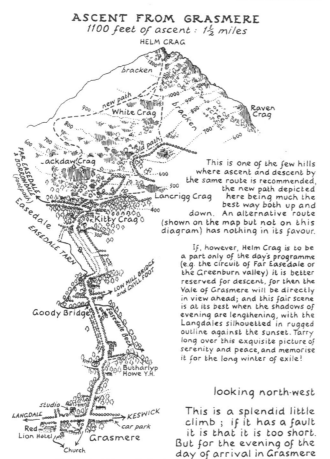

Helm Crag 4

ASCENT FROM GRASMERE
1100 feet of ascent : 1½ miles

HELM CRAG

bracken

new path

White Crag

Raven Crag

ackdaw Crag

FAR EASEDALE (BORROWDALE) (footpath)

Lancrigg Crag

Easedale

EASEDALE TARN

Kitty Crag

LOW MILL BRIDGE and GILL FOOT

Easedale Beck

Goody Bridge

Butharlyp Howe Y.H.

studio

LANGDALE

Red Lion Hotel

Grasmere

Church

KESWICK

car park

This is one of the few hills where ascent and descent by the same route is recommended, the new path depicted here being much the best way both up and down. An alternative route (shown on the map but not on this diagram) has nothing in its favour.

If, however, Helm Crag is to be a part only of the day's programme (e.g. the circuit of Far Easedale or the Greenburn valley) it is better reserved for descent, for then the Vale of Grasmere will be directly in view ahead; and this fair scene is at its best when the shadows of evening are lengthening, with the Langdales silhouetted in rugged outline against the sunset. Tarry long over this exquisite picture of serenity and peace, and memorise it for the long winter of exile!

looking north-west

This is a splendid little climb ; if it has a fault it is that it is too short. But for the evening of the day of arrival in Grasmere on a walking holiday it is just the thing : an epitome of Lakeland concentrated in the space of two hours — and an excellent foretaste of happy days to come.

From The Central Fells by A. Wainwright

on a rise to the left is Allan Bank, the least well known of Wordsworth's successive homes in the Lakes. He condemned it as an eyesore when it was being built, squarely in his view of Silver How from Dove Cottage, but in 1808 he moved here by boat across Grasmere lake, and spent two years as tenant. It was an eventful time, including a spell when Coleridge came to stay along with 500 books from the cluttered library of Thomas de Quincey, who had taken over from the Wordsworths at Dove Cottage. Scrupulous about returning borrowed books, Coleridge wrote 'Thomas de Quincey Esquire' in all 500. De Quincey recalls in his *Memories of the Lake Poets* how he and a girlfriend spent several weeks removing what he called 'the unnecessary heraldic addition' of 'esquire'. Rows with the landlord over smoking chimneys saw Wordsworth, his wife Mary and their five children move out in 1811, eventually to the grandeur of Rydal Mount, where the Wordsworths settled for more than 40 years. Allan Bank was later bought by Canon Hardwicke Rawnsley, who left it to the National Trust of which he was a co-founder.

The lane passes other large villas built for 19th-century worthies: Spelthorne, the holiday home of a Yorkshire carpet manufacturer Linton Taylor, who was a Quaker and bequeathed it as a guest house to be run by the Society of Friends so that others should enjoy the peace and beauty he had found. Lancrigg, in parkland with fine trees on the other side of the road, is where the Lake Poets used to meet. It now serves the same hospitable purpose as Spelthorne — and almost all other properties in Easedale — as a vegetarian hotel. A final stretch of tarmac runs unfenced across a large field, and the path then turns right and up a stony track between cottages to a gate amid trees.

Left is the walkers' highway up Far Easedale and over Greenup Edge to Borrowdale, another potential site of ramblers' traffic jams in high season as it forms part of Wainwright's Coast to Coast walk. Almost as many Coast to Coasters may be encountered on Helm Crag, though, as the fell marks the end (or beginning, if you are going east to west) of the walk's exhilarating high-level alternative to the Easedale track.

The path climbs quickly to an area of old quarries whose cliffs once diverted my young sons. One moment moping about the misery of having parents who wanted to do daft things like climb hills, the next they were crag-ratting up miniature rock faces and then circling us like inexhaustible collies all the way to the summit. From the quarries, an excellently engineered rock stairway has replaced the hopelessly eroded remains of the original path which went straight up this flank of Helm Crag. Instead, after steep steps between woodland and a wall, you are soon on a grassy shelf where the path switchbacks gently amid bracken, rowan and juniper trees and the occasional rock outcrop, with a satisfyingly steep cliff well to the left hand side. At the end, with fine views over the lonely upper reaches of Easedale, it hairpins to the right and up the wide shelf of grass with the wildflowers, plus increasingly inquisitive and picnic-savvy sheep.

At the top of this stretch, the path hooks round again, this time to the left, but divert a short way straight ahead to take in the lovely views of Grasmere and Wordsworth's little nook of mountain ground. Beyond is the trail of traffic on the A591 peering up at the Helm Crag knobbles. One of these is now you.

The Lion and the Lamb

The final stretch to the summit gets a little stonier as you climb and then, goodness, we suddenly find what the fuss Wainwright made about the summit is all about. A majestic scene of desolation starts with the Lion and the Lamb, two rocks which vaguely resemble these animals from certain angles at a distance in poor light, to the Howitzer, the angled barrel of rock which is the mountain's true top.

The path clings to the summit of the shattered ridge, with an easy alternative a few yards below to the left. Everything is perfectly safe but this is a cardinal place for obeying Wainwright's rule when walking on scree or boulders: watch your feet. It would be very easy to sprain or break an ankle here, proving Wainwright's otherwise rather debatable claim that all mountain accidents are the result of clumsiness. It is also safe and very interesting to scramble gingerly down into the small hanging valley below the ridge's rock formations, where the jumble of huge boulders provides plenty of shelter for alfresco lunching. On a third family climb up Helm Crag we found these invaluable to conceal the embarrassingly lavish picnic lunch provided by a top-end hotel in Grasmere, where we were having a birthday weekend. Each of us had a moulded plastic container of the sort in which airline food arrives for passengers in the posh seats. I am pretty sure that the first course was asparagus. We didn't dare tuck in in front of the cheese and tomato sandwich-eaters around the summit, so slunk off into one of the little caves.

The Howitzer

Try to outdo Wainwright on the Howitzer if you fancy it, but take great care. Otherwise, the top of Helm Crag is every bit as rewarding as it looks from below. You can play hide-and-seek and hunt for summer flowers which grow in the micro-climate of the most sheltered recesses even in winter. Trying to find the various fancifully named rock formations is another diversion. Which part of the jumble at the north-west end of the ridge can honestly be said to resemble an Old Woman Playing the Organ? It is also fascinating to potter beyond the first hanging valley below the ridge, above the Grasmere flank of Helm Crag. Only those who do, and climb over the parapet of rock which lies at the far side, will discover an unexpected second depression. This has a further protective parapet before the final, steep fall of the fellside amid stunted juniper trees to the dale below.

The whole summit landscape is both 'weird and fantastic', as Wainwright has it, and at the same time as apparently well planned as a medieval castle with successive lines of sturdy defence. Some immense volcanic convulsion or earth tremor aeons ago created all this magnificent mess. The entire crown of the mountain tilted and started to slide downhill but then stopped. Whatever the cause, the effect has been to create a memorable platform for us to gaze enraptured at views on all sides. Helvellyn and the Fairfield horseshoe rise beyond Grasmere. The vistas are equally grand up the valley towards Thirlmere and the ancient battleground of Dunmail Raise, and over the great, wild mass of mountains leading to and beyond the Langdale Pikes.

Greenup Edge

From the top of Helm Crag, a fine ridge walk mounts over Gibson Knott and Calf Crag to Greenup Edge, where the old packhorse route from Borrowdale can be used for a gentle descent back to Goody Bridge and Grasmere. Wainwright describes the steep, rough and craggy summit of this memorable mountain in Book Four, *The Central Fells*, as looking 'like a shaggy terrier in the company of sleek foxhounds'. Those who know his writing – or have read this book attentively – will know that this is praise indeed. He uses exactly the same simile one other time, three books later, in the final volume, *The Western Fells*: for his beloved Haystacks, his favourite in all of Lakeland, and the place where his ashes now lie.

THE LAKE DISTRICT can only benefit from more people learning about Alfred Wainwright and reading his books. He was well aware that the *Pictorial Guides* might bring many more people into the mountains where he so particularly liked to be alone, but he had good answers for that. It was inconceivable that someone whose whole life had been transformed by the beauty of the landscape could wish to deny it to others. And if visitors came with his words in their heads, indeed preferably in their hands, they would understand how to behave in a way which would in turn preserve the loveliness for future generations. Wainwright's followers do not wreck cairns or turn paths into scree scars or allow their dogs to worry sheep. Indeed, in the pleasantest way, they probably act as an informal force for good, keeping a watch on the fells.

Immersing yourself in his writings also leaves no doubt whatever that the guidebooks are not designed to turn free-spirited fellwanderers into little trams. You emphatically do not have to follow AW's dotted lines, even though Chris Jesty's revised editions are helpfully outlining them in red. Think of each route as a guide, not a rule. There are places where it would be madness to stray, such as Jack's Rake on Pavey Ark or the High Level and Shamrock traverses on Pillar; but most of the suggested ascents can be varied. Wainwright wants you to leave the beaten track.

Jesty's work is a splendid thing in itself, partly because his thousands of changes of detail do not detract from the essential Wainwright. All the wit and grumps and topographical curiosities are retained. At the time of writing (June 2007) he has completed up to Book Four, *The Southern Fells*, and the original Wainwrights are still in print too. The publisher of all seven *Pictorial Guides* and *The Outlying Fells of Lakeland* is Frances Lincoln, www.franceslincoln.com 4 Torriano Mews, Torriano Avenue, London, NW5 2RZ. They took over the entire Wainwright imprint as described in Chapter Two of this book, and have a feast of the great man's writing on offer including *The Coast to Coast Walk*, *The Pennine Way* and *Memoirs of a*

Fellwanderer, the closest he got to an autobiography.

Wainwright is also extremely well served by his biographer Hunter Davies, a Cumbrian whose 1995 book *Wainwright*, revised for a new edition in 2002, first revealed the agonies and complications – and ultimately fulfilment and happiness – of AW's life. It does so in a thorough and unsensationalist way, sympathetic but not hiding the darker side. Subsequent accounts, including Chapter One of this book, are greatly indebted to it as the central work, Wainwright's own books excluded, in the archive.

Davies gave the first Wainwright Memorial Lecture in 2003 to the Wainwright Society, an organisation which is not as obsessive as it may sound. Under the chairmanship of Eric Robson, another noted Lakeland writer and broadcaster, members promote, explore and generally celebrate their hero. In the process, as with the *Pictorial Guides*, the Lake District benefits enormously. The society has an excellent website, www.wainwright.org.uk, or may be contacted at The Wainwright Society, Kendal Museum, Station Road, Kendal, Cumbria LA9 6BT.

The museum is also the home of the Wainwright gallery, a display which would have tickled the town's former Borough Treasurer (and honorary curator of the museum) because part of it is devoted to a collection of ancient Egyptian funerary objects, and items such as a barometer belonging to the Manchester scientist John Dalton. There is, however, also a good collection of Wainwright's original drawings and handwritten pages from the guides, a mock-up of his Town Hall office and personal effects including his walking jacket, spectacles, rucksack, heavily darned socks and pipe. www.kendalmuseum.org.uk.

Anywhere and everywhere in the Lake District may be considered a shrine to Wainwright, but the top of Haystacks is clearly supreme. You can either go there, or gaze at the crumpled, enticing summit from the little one-storey St James' church in Buttermere, where a stone tablet in his memory is set into the sill below the south-west window which looks out and up towards the fell.

This book is published to accompany the television series
Wainwright: The Man Who Loved the Lakes, and Wainwright
Walks, produced by Skyworks and first broadcast on BBC
Four in 2007.

3 5 7 9 10 8 6 4

Published in 2007 by BBC Books, an imprint of Ebury
Publishing. Ebury Publishing is a Random House Group
Company.

The Random House Group Limited Reg. No. 954009.
Addresses for companies within the Random House Group
can be found at www.randomhouse.co.uk

A CIP catalogue record for this book is available from the
British Library.

ISBN 978 1 84607 294 9

The Random House Group Limited makes every effort to
ensure that the papers used in our books are made from
trees that have been legally sourced from well-managed and
credibly certified forests. Our paper procurement policy can
be found at www.randomhouse.co.uk

Commissioning editor: Mathew Clayton
Project editor: Steve Tribe
Copy-editor: Mike Evans
Designed by: Oil Often
Production controller: Antony Heller
Printed and bound by Appl Druck, Wemding, Germany

To buy books by your favourite authors and register for
offers, visit www.rbooks.co.uk

Pages and covers from the Pictorial Guides to the Lakeland
Fells and other publications are © A Wainwright and are
reproduced by kind permission of the Wainwright Estate and
Frances Lincoln Ltd

Photo credits:
Michael Sayles: pages 1, 2, 8, 12, 36, 58, 74, 83, 108, 112,
118, 128, 130, 148, 154, 160, 166, 172, 178 and 192
Rob Grange: pages 4, 18, 23, 26, 30, 32, 42, 48, 54, 56,
60, 64, 86, 90, 114, 122, 136, 142 and 169
Homer Sykes Archive/Alamy: page 6, 21 and 25
Derry Brabs: pages 10, 11 (right), 17 (right), 52, 62, 70
and 98
Aimie Wright: pages 44, 126 and 184
All other photographs by Richard Mervyn/Skyworks

Skyworks would like to thank Alfred Wainwright's wife,
Betty, and her daughter, Jane King – trustee of the
Wainwright Estate – for their commitment to the series, Eric
Robson and Hunter Davies for all their expert consultation
and guidance, the National Trust, Richard Mervyn for
capturing such spectacular imagery from his helicopter, all
the production team who worked so hard to bring the walks
and the documentary to the TV screens, Julia Bradbury for
her tremendous work throughout, and Richard Klein, for all
his encouragement and support from the BBC.